FRANCIS

People of God

Remarkable Lives, Heroes of Faith

People of God is a series of inspiring biographies for the general reader. Each volume offers a compelling and honest narrative of the life of an important twentieth- or twenty-first-century Catholic. Some living and some now deceased, each of these women and men has known challenges and weaknesses familiar to most of us but responded to them in ways that call us to our own forms of heroism. Each offers a credible and concrete witness of faith, hope, and love to people of our own day.

John XXIII	Massimo Faggioli
Oscar Romero	Kevin Clarke
Thomas Merton	Michael W. Higgins
Megan Rice	Dennis Coday
Francis	Michael Collins
Flannery O'Connor	Angela O'Donnell
Martin Sheen	Rose Pacatte
Jean Vanier	Michael W. Higgins
Dorothy Day	Patrick Jordan
Luis Antonio Tagle	Cindy Wooden

More titles to follow

Francis

Bishop of Rome

SECOND EDITION

Michael Collins

LITURGICAL PRESS
Collegeville, Minnesota
www.litpress.org

Cover design by Stefan Killen Design. Cover illustration by Philip Bannister.

1   2   3   4   5   6   7   8   9

Library of Congress Control Number: 2014942289

ISBN 978-0-8146-3705-0   978-0-8146-3730-2 (ebook)

Contents

Chapter One
Beginnings   1

Chapter Two
The Society of Jesus   13

Chapter Three
Bishop of Buenos Aires   30

Chapter Four
The First Conclave   64

Chapter Five
The Benedict Years   69

Chapter Six
The Abdication   74

Chapter Seven
The Second Conclave   84

Chapter Eight
A Pontificate Begins   93

Notes   137

Index   140

CHAPTER ONE

Beginnings

High above the Atlantic the cardinal archbishop of Buenos Aires slumbered. Halfway through the thirteen-hour flight from the Argentinian capital of Buenos Aires to Rome lights were dimmed and Cardinal Bergoglio closed his eyes. The past three weeks had been eventful. On February 11, 2013, Pope Benedict XVI had announced that he would resign the papal office on the last day of February. The cardinals had been summoned to Rome to elect his successor. As the seventy-six-year-old Cardinal Bergoglio crossed the sky, his thoughts may have turned to the sea voyage made by his father, Giovanni Mario, just seventy-seven years earlier when the young man had sailed from Italy with his parents to his new home in Argentina.

Cardinal Bergoglio's grandfather, Giovanni Bergoglio, was born on August 13, 1884, in the countryside of Asti in Bricco Marmorito in Valleversa. The house, set on a hilltop and surrounded by vineyards, had been purchased by four Bergoglio brothers from a Jewish vendor in 1854. Over the years the family had expanded. Some remained working on the land while others moved into commerce. One of the

1

brothers, Francesco, great-grandfather of the future pope, had married Maria Teresa Bugnano of San Martino al Tanaro. The young Bergoglio was baptized in the local Church of St. Bartholomew. He attended the state school at nearby Portocomara and during the summer holidays worked on the farm at Bricco Marmorito from which the family made a modest living.

On January 1, 1906, with the permission of his father, Giovanni traveled to Turin to begin a new life in the city. Shortly after his arrival he met a young girl of his own age, Rosa Vasallo, a native of Piano Crixia, a small town of 1,487 inhabitants that lay 30 miles west of Genoa. Rosa had also migrated to the city in the hope of improving her fortune. The two were soon engaged and were married the following year on August 20, 1907. On April 2, 1908, a son was born to the couple and was baptized Mario Bergoglio.

After ten years in Turin, Giovanni decided to return with his family to Asti. Work had been precarious in Turin, and Giovanni and Rosa decided that Asti offered better possibilities. On July 8, 1918, the family took up residence in No. 6 Antica Zecca. Giovanni found work as a barman in the vicinity. Within a couple of years a new opportunity opened when he became the porter and security man in charge of a private clinic in Via Massimo d' Azeglio, which also included rent-free accommodation. With money saved from having to pay rent the young couple was able to move once more, and in 1923 Giovanni and Rosa took up residence at No. 14 Corso Alessandria where they opened a grocery store.

Rosa was a devout young woman, intensely proud of her Catholic faith. Both Giovanni and Rosa joined Catholic Action, a lay group that tried to influence society with Catholic values. By 1923 Rosa, now aged thirty-nine, was appointed as councillor, offering guidance for young people in the movement. On June 8 the following year she spoke at the annual conference of Catholic Action and with the encouragement of the chaplain, Don Luigi Goria, she traveled throughout the province addressing local branches. The young Mario inherited a strong faith, particularly from his mother. In November 1925 at the age of seventeen, Mario gave an impassioned discourse on the papacy at a meeting of the Federation of the Diocesan Youth of Turin in the parish of San Martino.

Giovanni and Rosa were ambitious for their only child. Making financial sacrifices the couple sent Mario to study accounting in Turin, a rare profession for the son of a farmer at the time. To the satisfaction of his parents Mario qualified as an accountant at the age of nineteen.

With the rise of Fascism in Italy during the 1920s, Giovanni and Rosa discussed the possibility of emigrating. Already family members and friends of the extended family had migrated, many of whom had chosen Argentina as their new home.

The Fascist political party was founded in 1919 by an Italian soldier, Benito Mussolini. By mid-1922 the party had gained a considerable number of supporters who had been disillusioned by the financial collapse of Italy following the First World War. The Fascists took advantage of the general malaise in the economy and seized political power when the opportunity arose.

Many Italians believed that migration was preferable to living in an impoverished state under political rulers in whom they had no trust. Already in 1927 Giovanni and Rosa had made the decision to migrate. Through a series of letters from relatives in Argentina they were assured that a warm welcome awaited them and that their financial situation would improve. Three of Giovanni's brothers had already emigrated and settled in Argentina. With Giovanni's departure only one brother and sister would remain in Italy.

Passage was arranged to Buenos Aires on the *Principessa Mafalda*. On October 25, 1927, the transatlantic ocean liner sank off the coast of Brazil. Of the more than 1,200 passengers aboard 314 drowned. Following the tragedy, many prospective passengers delayed their departure on long-distance liners. The Bergoglios had booked their tickets but were unable to travel as the sale of their shop had not been completed and they lacked emigration documents. This inconvenience may have saved their lives.

Argentina had become a welcoming haven for thousands of European migrants who hoped to make a new life in a climate similar to their continent of origin. Article 25 of the 1853 constitution acknowledges the importance of migration and offered a welcome to those who decided to settle in the country: "Federal Government will encourage European immigration and it will not restrict, limit or burden with any taxes the entrance into Argentinian territory of foreigners who come with the goal of working the land, improving the industries and teaching the sciences and the arts."

In the first half of the twentieth century the population of Argentina doubled. Between 1914 and 1947 the population rose from 7.9 million to 15.8 million. The largest number of settlers in the New World came from Spain, Portugal, and Italy.

In early 1929 Giovanni, Rosa, and their twenty-four-year-old son set sail on the transatlantic ocean liner *Giulio Caesare* bound for Argentina. On February 15 the ship docked in the port of Buenos Aires. Although the weather was unseasonably warm, Rosa wore a long coat with a fur collar. Inside the lining of the collar she had stitched Italian lire, the total sum of the family's savings that she had smuggled out of Italy. With relief she passed through the customs office without being noticed or questioned. The money hidden away in Rosa's collar would be enough to allow the family to make a new start in Argentina.

South America would be their homeland for the rest of their lives. Work was plentiful, civil strife was rare, and social prospects were good. Early twentieth-century Buenos Aires was the largest conurbation after London and New York.

Following a brief sojourn in Buenos Aires the Bergoglios proceeded to the nearby province of Paraná, where since 1922 the Bergoglio brothers had run a successful paving company. With his accountancy skills Mario proved a welcome addition to the family business.

The Bergoglios easily settled into their new surroundings and lived in the large apartment block that the brothers had built some years earlier. But their fortunes changed for the worse following the sudden collapse of the building industry in 1932 caused by the Wall Street Crash of 1929.

The Bergoglios were obliged to sell the house in which they lived. Even the family tomb had to be sold. One of the three brothers, the head of the paving firm, died from cancer, and another brother borrowed two thousand pesos in order to buy a store and some stock. Through hard work and determination the brothers managed to survive the crisis although they were unable to revive entirely the family fortunes.

Shortly afterward, Giovanni, Rosa, and Mario moved to Buenos Aires in the hope of finding new work, settling in the area of Flores, which was popular with migrants from the north of Italy.

In 1934 Mario met his future wife, Regina María Sivori, ten years his junior, at a social function in the parish of San Antonio in Almagro. Following a brief engagement the couple was married in the local church on December 12, 1935.

The newlyweds bought a small house in the district of Flores, close to Plaza de la Misericordia. In this home the couple's five children would be reared.

On December 17, 1936, Regina María gave birth to her firstborn. He was christened Jorge, a name frequently used within the family. A week later on Christmas Day, the infant was baptized in the Basilica of San Carlos Borromeo by the Salesian priest Fr. Enrique Pozzoli, who was to have a great influence on young Jorge and who later became the youth's spiritual director. The infant's godparents were his uncle Francisco Sivori and his grandmother Rosa Vassallo de Bergoglio.

When Jorge was just thirteen months old his mother gave birth to a second son, Alberto Horacio. With another infant in the house, Regina María needed help. The expanding family could not afford assistance, and Rosa was eager to help her daughter-in-law. Each day Rosa went to collect her grandson and took the infant to her house. There she fed and cared for him until the evening when he was returned to his parents. As a very young child Jorge learned Italian at his grandmother's knee. His grandparents and his uncles spoke the Piedmontese dialect among themselves. It was the language of a faraway land that belonged in the past. The young child noted the tinge of nostalgia in their voices as they spoke of people he had never heard of and whom they never would see again. It was during these years that Jorge formed a deep attachment to his grandmother.

The church, administered by the Salesian Order, played an important role in the lives of the large Italian community, especially migrants from Turin and the surrounding area. There were regular church services and annual feast days and processions. The great songwriter, actor, and proponent of the tango, Carlos Gardel, sang in the choir as a youth. Another notable past member of the parish choir was the native Indian of Patagonia, Blessed Ceferino Namuncurá, a Salesian seminarian who died in 1905.

Years later Jorge would have reason to appreciate the Italian language he had learned from his older relatives. His father, however, had little interest in maintaining the old language or traditions. Although Mario spoke Spanish with a lilting Italian accent, he regarded himself as Argentinian and always spoke Castilian Spanish with his children. Bedtime stories however were usually tales from Italy or from the Bible.

Jorge's early education was at the nearby San Juan Bosco school on Calle Varela and later at the Salesian school on Avenida de Mayo 1800 in Ramos Mejía. Throughout his life he retained a special affection for the Salesian nuns who taught him. As a priest and later as bishop he always returned once a year to celebrate Mass for the community.

Rosa had an enormous influence on her grandchildren. She told them stories about her homeland and recounted how once she had mounted a pulpit in the local church to denounce Mussolini. She told them fables and tales from Italy, a land that seemed quite magical to them. Speaking decades later to Fr. Juan Isasmendi on the parish radio of Villa 21, Jorge recalled, "The one who had the greatest impact on me was my grandmother, who taught me the faith and read me the lives of the saints." Many years later as his grandmother was dying in a nursing home run by the Camillan Sisters, Jorge faithfully visited her most days. "This is the most important moment of her life," he told one of the sisters as he held his grandmother's hand. "She is going before the Lord."

Life for the Bergoglio family was similar to that of most of their neighbors. The presence of a large number of Italian migrants helped preserve traditions from their homeland

and forge new alliances. There were problems of integration, finding jobs, and keeping contact by letter and telegrams with family back home. Mario found work in the administration of a hosiery factory and later in the accounting department of the state railroads, which assured him of a reasonable living. Both parents loved music. The family regularly listened to the gramophone, and on Saturday afternoons Regina and the children gathered around the radio to listen to a broadcast of opera.

At weekends Jorge attended football matches played by the local club, San Lorenzo de Almagro, which was founded in 1908 at the nearby chapel of Saint Anthony by the Salesian priest Fr. Lorenzo Massa. The club was at the center of the sporting life of the district. Father Massa had started the club after a young boy was killed by a passing tram while he was playing on the street.

Mario was a passionate supporter of the club and played basketball there. The young Jorge also learned to play basketball and football and remained a lifelong fan of the San Lorenzo club, with its red and blue striped jersey.

Mario and Regina María had five children—Jorge, Alberto Horacio, Oscar Adrian, Marta Regina, and María Elena—all of whom were born within ten years. Before the birth of her last born, Regina María had suffered a miscarriage. With the birth of her fifth child, Regina María was temporarily paralyzed. Although a woman came three times a week to help with the laundry and some household chores, the children were required to help around the house. As the eldest, Jorge learned to cook during this time. His mother measured out the ingredients while he boiled the water and prepared the food.

Although the Bergoglios did not possess a car or take summer vacations, the family was relatively well-off. Jorge was surprised by his father's insistence that he begin part-time work when he was thirteen. Through his father's contacts he got a job cleaning at the Hickthier–Bachmann hosiery factory.

Jorge worked each day from 7:00 a.m. until 1:00 p.m. After two years, at the age of fifteen, he entered the administration area. While maintaining the part-time job Jorge continued with his schooling at the Escuela Nacional de Educación Técnica, dividing his time between study and work. While he continued to begin work early each morning, he was obliged to attend lectures until 8:00 p.m.

In retrospect Jorge was grateful to his father for his insistence that he both work and study. Meeting so many unemployed people he realized that work is not simply an obligation but also taught him to value money and to avoid waste and excess.

During these years he became an avid reader, in particular the works of Dante, Manzoni, and Hölderlin. His work supervisor at the factory, Esther Balarino de Careaga from Paraguay, was an ardent Communist and it was through her that he became familiar with Communist thought despite the fact that Communism was condemned by the church as an atheistic worldview. Although he did not become a Communist, Jorge was influenced by the philosophy of several Communist writers. Some years later during civil unrest of the 1970s, Jorge learned that Esther's daughter and son-in-law were abducted, and she herself was kidnapped along with two nuns. She later died in captivity following severe torture.

Throughout his teenage years Jorge was interested in social work and joined the local branch of Catholic Action in which his parents had been active in Italy. Although a shy youth he mixed easily within his circle of friends.

At the age of seventeen Jorge had an intense spiritual experience that he regarded as a turning point in his life. On September 21, 1953, the first day of Argentinian spring, Jorge and a group of companions decided to go for a picnic. It was a traditional day for young people to congregate and spend time together. On his way to the gathering, Jorge stopped at the local church of San Jose de Flores. Fr. Duarte was preaching, and Jorge waited to meet him and asked the priest to hear his confession. It was during this dialogue that Jorge raised the question of a vocation to the priesthood for the first time. Half a century later he recounted some details of the encounter: "Something strange happened to me in that confession. I don't know what it was, but it changed my life. I think it surprised me, caught me with my guard down. . . . From that moment on, for me, God is the One who *te primerea*—'springs it on you.' You search for Him, but He finds you first."[1]

Although he thought about becoming a priest he was undecided on what order or diocese he should enter. He continued to study more and pray about a possible vocation. Four years passed before he finally made up his mind to try his religious vocation.

When he was twenty-one Jorge decided to become a diocesan priest and enroll in the seminary. His plans were nearly thwarted when he was diagnosed with a severe form of pneumonia. Three cysts had appeared on the upper part of his lung. When he didn't respond to conventional medication, the decision was made to operate. The right lung was severely affected, and the surgeon removed the upper part of the organ. Following his recuperation he decided to pursue his vocation to the religious life. While his father was pleased with his son's decision, his mother was dismayed. She had discovered her son's decision indirectly and considered him too young and not yet mature enough to make such a choice. Regina María had cleared out a small area in the upper story of the house, overlooking a small terrace, where Jorge was able to study in peace. As the eldest, Jorge was looked up to by his siblings. They were told to be quiet while he was studying and sent to play outside.

One day, while dusting the area, Jorge's mother looked at the books her son was studying. She was surprised to find several books of theology. She had to wait until evening when he returned home to confront him on his choice of reading material. When he returned that evening, she asked why he had lied to her.

"I did not lie, Mama," replied Jorge. "I am studying medicine, but medicine of the soul."

To his surprise, Regina María reacted badly to the news of her son's vocation, realizing that soon he would leave home to study at a seminary. She continuously pleaded with him to delay his decision.

When he entered the archdiocesan seminary, Immaculada Concepción in Villa Devoto, Jorge had decided to become a diocesan priest and work in Buenos Aires. He loved his native city but he became drawn to spread the faith beyond his country as a missionary. For a period he considered becoming a Salesian priest, as he wanted to work with young people.

Inspired by Jesuit priests who assisted at the diocesan seminary, Jorge approached the vocations director for the order. After a period of reflection and with the permission of the rector, Jorge decided to join the Jesuit Order. As he explained in later years, he was particularly attracted to the sense of order and discipline evident in the Jesuit way of life, and in particular he wanted to leave for the mission territories, preferably Japan, where the Jesuits had an established an important presence.

On March 11, 1958, Jorge entered the Society of Jesus. After a brief preparation in Córdoba, Jorge traveled to Santiago, Chile, where he entered the novitiate. The following year he experienced the first great bereavement of his life when his father died of a sudden heart attack. The death of the head of the family caused Jorge immense grief as the two had been so close. His mother now had four children to look after and was unable to call on Jorge for assistance.

CHAPTER TWO

The Society of Jesus

The Society of Jesus, popularly called the Jesuits, was founded in 1540 by the Spaniard Ignatius of Loyola. For almost half a millennium it has been one of the most important and influential religious orders in the Catholic Church.

Ignatius, the youngest of thirteen children, was born on October 23, 1491, into a minor noble family at Azpeitia, a town in the northern Basque region of Spain. His mother died soon after his birth, and he was nursed by the daughter of the local blacksmith. At the age of seventeen, having trained as a page at the court of a relative, Juan Velázquez de Cuéllar, Ignatius entered the service of Antonio Manrique de Lara, the Duke of Nájera and the Viceroy of Navarre. This service prepared him for a military career.

The young man became a successful soldier and participated in a number of battles until he was seriously wounded during the siege of Pamplona in May 1521 when a cannonball injured both his legs and left him crippled.

During his long recuperation, Ignatius read a number of spiritual texts. After his recovery he made a pilgrimage of thanksgiving to the sanctuary of Our Lady of Montserrat near Barcelona. There on March 25, 1522, he left his sword and dagger as he embraced a new way of life. Rejecting his luxurious clothing and his military decorations, he adopted the simple black gown of a scholar. During the next ten months Ignatius lived in a cave at Manresa and began to formulate the Spiritual Exercises, one of the most famous spiritual treatises in sixteenth-century Europe. The following year, Ignatius traveled to the Holy Land to visit the places where Jesus had lived.

Returning to Spain, Ignatius devoted himself to the promotion and defense of the Catholic faith, sometimes preaching in the marketplace or squares of towns and villages. He studied at the universities of Alcalá and Salamanca before enrolling in theology lectures at the University of Paris in the summer of 1528.

During seven formative years in Paris, Ignatius made staunch friends among the student body. Six of these became close companions: a French and Portuguese student and four Spaniards.

The church was engaged in a crisis caused by the criticisms of a number of reformers. Martin Luther, John Calvin, Ulrich Zwingli, and other zealous Christians proposed dramatic action to excise corruption and hypocrisy in the Catholic Church.

The papacy was slow in reacting efficiently to the proposals of the reformers. Rather than accept the many valid criticisms, the pontiffs rejected their efforts and condemned their teachings. The tardy response not only delayed church reform but also led to decades of civil wars throughout Europe.

The six companions discussed ways of assisting their fellow Catholics to remain steadfast in their faith and refute heresy. On August 15, 1534, Ignatius and his companions attended Mass at the Church of Our Lady of the Martyrs at Montmartre in Paris where in the crypt they took vows, offering their lives for the defense of the Catholic faith.

In the succeeding years Ignatius struggled with poor health that made his enterprise all the more difficult. With his six companions he petitioned the pope for an audience in Rome. The companions wanted papal direction to found a religious order that would ensure the continuation of their apostolate.

Although he had been ordained in June 1537, Ignatius waited for more than a year before celebrating his first Mass on Christmas Day 1538 in the Basilica of St. Mary Major's in Rome. According to a pious legend, the church housed the manger in which Jesus was believed to have been born and had been brought to Rome centuries earlier.

In 1540 the society received papal recognition, and two years later Ignatius was elected general of the newly founded order. In addition to the traditional vows of poverty, chastity, and obedience, Ignatius and his followers took a fourth vow of fidelity to the pope. This fourth vow required the companions to put themselves at the disposal of the Roman pontiff and carry out any missions with which he may charge them, particularly the education of youth and missionary work.

A particular charism of the order is discernment. Members were urged by Ignatius to think carefully about their actions, taking care not to let their passions or prejudices affect their decisions. This aesthetic attitude became a hallmark of the fledgling order.

Although the society was properly known as the Society of Jesus, the term *Jesuit* was first used in 1544 in a derogatory manner. Ignatius never used the term himself as it mocked someone who employed the name of Jesus excessively in conversation. Gradually, however, the term was appropriated by the members and came to be used in a positive sense.

During the following decade, the Society of Jesus experienced rapid growth. The Jesuits were decisive in launching the Catholic Reformation, a response to the fracturing of the Christian faith in Europe. Many reformers had attacked the corruption in the papacy and the clergy in general. Within a few years, hundreds had joined the Company of Jesus. By the time of Ignatius's death in Rome in 1556, the members of the society were engaged in missions in Europe, India, China, and Japan. With particular dedication to the education of young people, the Jesuits set up schools and universities, raising the standard of education.

On March 12, 1622, Ignatius was canonized by Pope Gregory XV. For more than a century the Jesuits flourished, establishing educational academies and expanding missions in various lands. Toward the end of the eighteenth century, disaster struck the order.

In 1773 Pope Clement XIV issued a decree suppressing the Society of Jesus. The Jesuits had become numerous and powerful but had also gained many enemies who viewed them with suspicion and mistrust. Clement acceded to political pressure from several European countries, some of which desired to seize Jesuit assets.

While the order managed to survive in some countries such as Prussia, the widespread abolition was reversed by Pope Pius VII in 1814. In the period following the restoration, the influence of the Jesuits expanded once more. By the middle of the twentieth century the order had reached its numerical zenith.

During the post-Vatican II period, and especially under the pontificate of John Paul II, the Jesuits experienced tensions between the order and the papacy while religious organizations such as Opus Dei, Communion and Liberation, and the Legionaries of Christ found favor with the Polish pope.

The general of the Jesuits, Pedro Arrupe (1965–1983), refocused the order, emphasizing the members' care for the poor. This "option for the poor" was most notable in the work of the South American Jesuits. In some places their work provoked violent opposition. On November 16, 1989, six Jesuits, along with a housekeeper and her daughter, were murdered by the military on the campus of the Central American University in El Salvador.

Today the Jesuits form the largest single religious order in the Catholic Church, numbering more than 17,000 members dispersed throughout 119 countries on six continents. Their work has diversified to schools and universities, hospitals and scientific research, culture, and communications.

Ignatius's initial vision for his clerics was one of military discipline. Part of the charism is the successful manner in which members are enabled to retain their individuality and foster their unique talents. In recent years the Jesuits have worked closely with a growing number of volunteers, people attracted by Ignatian spirituality and drawn to work in various Jesuit projects, especially in the area of social justice.

Since Jesuits make a promise not to seek promotion within the church, it is rare to find Jesuits in senior ranks of the clergy, in particular the episcopate. This vow, however, also entails accepting such positions when required by church authorities. At the time of his election to the papacy, Jorge Bergoglio was one of six living Jesuit cardinals. Over almost five hundred years, there have been some fifty cardinals chosen from the Society of Jesus.

Jesuit training lasts between eight and fourteen years, depending on the previous educational achievements of the novice. During the novitiate in Chile, the main emphasis for Bergoglio and his classmates was the study of Ignatian spirituality and the experience of the full thirty-day Spiritual Exercises. In addition the novices studied Latin, Greek, history, and literature. On March 12, 1960, Bergoglio and his companions took the first vows of poverty, chastity, and obedience. Bergoglio was assigned to teach literature and psychology at the Colegio de la Immaculada, a secondary school in Santa Fé. There, he taught courses from 1964 to 1965 before moving to the Colegio del Salvador in Buenos Aires in 1966. As chemistry was his specialty, Bergoglio was surprised when his superiors assigned him to teach humanities at the school run by the order. While he found basic psychology easy to teach, the course on literature presented problems.

Although Bergoglio had developed a passion for literature, his students were less enthused. A meticulous teacher, he nonetheless found it difficult to engage the class. Many of his students recalled his self-discipline and strictness, although he brought outsiders such as Jorge Luis Borge to lecture to the students.

Jorge Bergoglio was ordained a priest on December 13, 1969, four days before his thirty-third birthday, by Archbishop Ramón José Castellano. His mother, siblings, and members of his family attended the ceremony, which was followed by a reception for all the newly ordained priests. A number of his former schoolteachers were also guests.

Immediately following his ordination, Bergoglio concluded his studies at San José Seminary before he and some companions were sent to Madrid, a city of some two hundred thousand inhabitants, to continue their formation within the society at the Jesuit house associated with the sixteenth-century University of Alcalá de Henares de Madrid. This period of spiritual formation is known within the order as *tertianship*.

This was Bergoglio's first visit to Europe, the continent of his ancestors. The church was still in the first flush of enthusiasm following the Second Vatican Council. Convened by Pope John XXIII in 1962–65, the Second Vatican

Council was the first global gathering of the church's bishops in almost a century. Over the course of sixteen centuries, twenty ecumenical councils had discussed issues pertaining to Christian life. During major sessions and smaller working commissions, the bishops discussed controversial issues facing the contemporary church.

The goal of the council was to find methods to make the Christian message adaptable to the world less than two decades after the Second World War and during the era of the Cold War. The bishops tried to establish closer links between other Christians and members of the world's faiths. The council dealt with a number of internal ecclesiastical issues such as missionary work, the role of the laity in the church, the nature of the ordained ministry, and the language and celebration of the sacraments. The council also discussed improvements in Catholic education and development in social issues.

In 1968, three years after the end of the council, Pope Paul VI issued the encyclical *Humanae Vitae* on the dignity of life. Although an insightful document, the issue that caught public attention was the general prohibition on artificial contraception. Many clergy had expected a change in the law on obligatory celibacy, even though the bishops had never indicated waiving the rule.

The postconciliar years were filled with hope and frustration, renewed energy and optimism, as well as disillusionment. These were the years in which Jorge Bergoglio and his companions were ordained and began their ministry.

In 1972 Bergoglio returned to Argentina to take charge of the Jesuit novitiate at Villa Barilari in San Miguel. He was strict on the novices, insisting that they do their own laundry, work in the garden, and cook in the kitchen. He himself participated in all the household chores. Above all he did not tolerate waste, insisting that food left over from one meal to the other would eventually be consumed. This attitude failed to make him popular among the novices.

On April 22, 1973, Fr. Jorge Bergoglio made his perpetual profession. Now a fully formed Jesuit he was appointed rector of the Colegio Máximo and lecturer in the faculty of theology. At the same time he was named a consultor for the province of the Jesuits. It was a rapid promotion but one which was to be superseded in a more dramatic fashion. On July 13, 1973, the Jesuit General Pedro Arrupe appointed Bergoglio as the new provincial. This event dramatically changed Bergoglio's life and his relationship with his fellow Jesuits both in Argentina and abroad. In that same year Arupe summoned Jesuit provincials to a meeting in Rome where he outlined a shift in favor of the poor.

The Jesuit Order is governed from Rome by the superior general and a council of advisers. Globally the order is divided into provinces, each overseen by a provincial. Assisted by a socius, or general adviser, the provincial oversees the Jesuits in his territory, appointing rectors to houses and directors for colleges and other apostolates. The provincial acts as a local link between the general based in Rome and the members of the order in a particular country or territory. The Argentinian province at the time consisted of fifteen houses, 166 priests, thirty-two brothers, and twenty students.

In the immediate aftermath of the Second Vatican Council, the Jesuit Order suffered an abrupt decline. Bergoglio was appointed provincial to succeed Fr. Richard O'Farrell who had only served four years of his six-year term. The Argentinian province was in turmoil, and the Jesuit curia in Rome decided to intervene before things deteriorated further.

Argentina was not immune to the fall in numbers, and as provincial Jorge Bergoglio traveled regularly from his base at Colegio Máximo to the various schools, religious houses, and social projects run by the Jesuits throughout Argentina.

From the beginning Bergoglio found himself the head of a bitterly divided province. Those who were loyal to O'Farrell resented the arrival of the newly professed Jesuit. Although he had been in the order for fourteen years, many viewed Bergoglio as young and inexperienced, a view Bergoglio himself came to share years later. Several Jesuits abandoned the traditional role of teaching in favor of caring for the poor in slum areas. Bergoglio insisted that they remain faithful to their original charism. Those who advocated changes in the liturgy and traditional religious life found the provincial unsympathetic and unwilling to compromise. For the first time many Jesuit confreres came to see Bergoglio as stubborn and unreasonable. While experimentation in the liturgy was widespread, Bergoglio insisted on retaining the traditional liturgy and devotional practices, favoring Gregorian chant over modern compositions, many by fellow Jesuits.

If the first three years of his mandate were stressful due to tensions within the order, the second three years of Bergoglio's period in office coincided with the most brutal period of civil unrest that engulfed Argentina.

In the decades following the Second World War several countries in South America were caught up in the so-called Cold War. The clash between communist and capitalist ideologies in the region led to the establishment of right-wing dictatorships. Some of these were granted military and financial support from the United States. In particular, the Americans were determined to keep Soviet influence from infiltrating their country.

The twentieth century saw six military coups in Argentina. The first occurred in 1930 and the last took place in 1976. Fourteen dictators were imposed between 1930 and the end of the dictatorship in 1983. Following the 1976 coup, which overthrew President Isabel Perón, General Jorge Videla became de facto president of Argentina, at the head of a military junta. His reign was marked by violent repression of political opponents.

Videla was determined to destroy both right-wing and leftist groups that used violent methods against the government. The People's Revolutionary Army was the armed wing of the Worker's Revolutionary Party. The Montonero Perónista Movement was a leftist guerrilla group determined to undermine fascist governments by terror and violence. Many of the members recruited from Catholic universities and other church groups saw the violence as an unavoidable part of the class struggle that would eventually win freedom and respect for human rights.

In 1970 the Montoneros had kidnapped and executed Pedro Aramburo, the dictator who had ruled from 1955 to 1958. In 1972 the group planted a bomb at the Sheraton Hotel. The following year Colonel Héctor Irabarren was killed while resisting a kidnap attempt. The Montoneros encouraged the former president, the socialist Juan Perón to return from his seventeen-year exile in Madrid to lead the country once more. When Perón returned to Argentina, the group was split over his policies to end unemployment and improve social justice. With Perón's death in 1974, his widow Isabel took over the leadership of the country. Despite her enormous popularity she was unable to stop the violence and killings that multiplied during her presidency. Isabel Perón signed laws allowing Videla to act decisively to destroy the opposition.

While combating the Marxist-inspired groups the government was supported by the Argentine Anticommunist Alliance founded in 1973 and led by José López Rega. The right-wing party sought to do away with all opposition to the governing powers, eliminating journalists, leftist guerrillas, union leaders, students, intellectuals, nuns, and priests engaged with the poor, and all other dissidents. During the period of unrest many priests and religious sisters and brothers became engaged in the struggle to obtain human rights for the poorly educated, the unemployed, and the disenfranchised.

Despite the natural resources of South America and the Caribbean islands, poverty remains an inescapable reality. Centuries of exploitation by Spain and Portugal in the slave trade, corrupt foreign administrators, and incompetent rulers reduced much of the population to poverty. Contemporary Argentina has suffered from decades of military and democratically elected rulers who have failed to adequately advance the nation's prosperity and take advantage of its natural resources.

Corresponding to the political upheaval during the 1960s and 1970s, some church leaders began to challenge the status quo, protesting the exploitation of the poor and examining the structures that both led them into poverty and disenfranchised them. A number of writers reached an ever-widening audience about the injustice of such social structures. One such writer, the Peruvian Dominican priest Gustavo Gutiérrez, wrote a number of books, arguing that the obligation to eradicate poverty lies with the educated and those who have resources. His seminal work, *A Theology of Liberation*, was published in 1971 and immediately gained a wide audience. Gutiérrez wrote with authority. His mixed ancestry included native Quechua and colonial Spanish blood. "Poverty is not a fate," Gutiérrez argued, "it is a condition, not a destiny; an injustice, not a misfortune. . . . Poverty is the result of the way society has been organized, in its diverse manifestations."[1]

Thus Christian engagement with the poor is not a choice, he claimed, it is an obligation. The Christian is not called to share what is left over but rather to share equally, treating other humans with respect. Above all, it means channeling energies and talents on behalf of the needy. It is Christian solidarity and lies at the heart of the Gospel message.

The bishops of Latin America were deeply aware of the plight of their people, although they were divided as to the best manner in which to help. Some bishops tried to create just structures for society, protecting and promoting human rights. Others were less interested in these issues and maintained their diocese without change.

In 1968 the bishops of Latin America met in the Colombian city of Medellín. The Second Vatican Council, which several Latin bishops had attended, had closed three years earlier. The positive energy and enthusiasm that the council had engendered permeated the meeting at Medellín. In their concluding document the bishops identified the "institutionalized violence" of poverty and challenged both governments and people to change the political systems that denied the poor access to a basic standard of living, better medical care, and the right to work. Although not all the bishops were in favor of provoking governments, the bishops' united statement had an immediate impact.

Four years later, in 1972, the bishops met again. During the meeting they voted Colombian Bishop Alfonso López Trujillo to the position of secretary general. López Trujillo, who had close connections to the Vatican, convinced several bishops to withdraw their tacit support for the revolutionary theology. The similarity of Karl Marx's analysis of poverty and some theologians' interpretation was seen as too close.

Pope John Paul II traveled to the Mexican city of Puebla in January 1979 to open the Third General Conference of the Latin American bishops. In a lengthy address he under-lined that the church's main mission is to preach the Gospel and thinly warned against the developments of recent years:

> People claim to show Jesus as politically committed, as one who fought against Roman oppression and the authorities, and also as one involved in the class struggle. This idea of Christ as a political figure, a revolutionary, as the subver-sive man from Nazareth, does not tally with the Church's catechesis. By confusing the insidious pretexts of Jesus' accusers with the—very different—attitude of Jesus him-self, some people adduce as the cause of his death the outcome of a political conflict, and nothing is said of the Lord's will to deliver himself and of his consciousness of his redemptive mission.[2]

Such staunch opposition derived from John Paul's experi-ence of communist Poland, which he had left four months earlier, following his election to the papacy. His struggle against the Polish authorities was still uppermost in his mind.

The proponents of liberation theology argued that the world of Latin America was quite different. John Paul had no direct experience of the region and depended on advisers such as López Trujillo whom he asked to draft the address. Not all bishops supported the secretary general's views.

Bergoglio, understanding the motivation of his confreres engaged in promoting social justice, took a cautious ap-proach, based on previous experience, and urged those under his authority to avoid open conflict with government agents.

In May 1976, two Jesuit priests, Orlando Yorio and Fran-cisco Jalics, were arrested by military police. They had pre-viously asked Archbishop Aramburo and Jorge Bergoglio for permission to live in the slum areas while teaching at the university. Bergoglio was opposed to their requests on two grounds. First, he did not agree with their work in the slums, and, second, he did not believe they were safe. Although the two men were older than Bergoglio and had taught him, Bergoglio instructed them to obey his orders and earlier in February 1973 had closed their community. Bergoglio's stubborn insistence split the Jesuits in Argentina ever more deeply and both Yorio and Jalics contemplated leaving the Jesuit Order in March of that year and founding a new congregation.

Once they were arrested, the two priests were kept illegally, blindfolded and handcuffed, and mistreated for five months. During the sessions, the captors told them that it was Bergoglio who had betrayed them.

In 2000 Fr. Francisco Jalics met Bergoglio and discussed their past differences. Bergoglio tried to convince him that he had actively sought the release of his confreres. On March 20, 2013, seven days after Jorge Bergoglio's election as pope, Jalics published a clarification of the events surrounding the kidnapping: "I myself was once inclined to believe that we were the victims of a denunciation. At the end of the 1990s, after numerous conversations, it became clear to me that this suspicion was unfounded. It is therefore wrong to assert that our capture took place at the initiative of Fr. Bergoglio."[3]

Yorio continued to blame Bergoglio. He left Argentina in 1992 and refused to forgive him right until his death in 2000.

Bergoglio himself recalled the events when summoned to a court in 2011. The mandate of the court was to discover the truth about those years.

"I did what I could for my age," he recalled, "and, with the few contacts I had, to plead for people who had been kidnapped."[4]

Despite his limited contacts, Bergoglio managed to persuade a military chaplain to allow him to take his place at a celebration Mass attended by the dictator Videla where he used the opportunity to request information about the two priests. Other bishops who also pleaded for the "disappeared," were equally unsuccessful. After five months the two priests were released and Bergoglio later claimed that this was in part due to his intercession.

During his period as provincial, Bergoglio regularly sheltered people at the college who were in hiding from the military police. Several fled the country, and on one occasion Bergoglio gave a man who resembled him his identity card and clerical garb to make his escape.

As provincial, Bergoglio insisted the Jesuits serve in parishes that had either been founded by the congregation or work in traditional diocesan parishes. He distrusted the growing "base communities" where there was little hierarchical supervision. In particular he was suspicious of anybody who used Marxist thought in analyzing the agony of the poor and those neglected by society at large. Only when he became bishop in Buenos Aires and had direct contact with the people in the shantytowns did he change to become a champion of the parish system adopted by the "slum priests."

In 1980 following his term of office as provincial, Bergoglio returned to the academic life as rector of Colegio Máximo de San José. The college was the faculty of philosophy and theology. Many Jesuits gave a relieved welcome to Fr. Andres Swindon when he replaced Bergoglio as provincial. Bergoglio's new position removed him from any influence among the central administration of the Jesuits. His wounds were still healing, but Bergoglio seemed oblivious to the division that he had caused during his six-year period as provincial. He had found the term more demanding than he had expected and was glad to move on to another appointment within the order.

In preparation for his new role, Bergoglio traveled to Ireland where he spent the months of June and July, living in the Jesuit community at Milltown Park in Dublin. It was partly a sabbatical period but he spent the time learning English.

On January 9 the following year his mother suffered a fatal heart attack in Buenos Aires.

Life as rector was relatively tranquil. He enjoyed lecturing but he also served in the parish of San José, in the district of San Miguel. Some saw these years as an exile but Bergoglio largely recalled them with affection, especially his work in the parish of San José de San Miguel where he taught catechism. In 1986 Bergoglio finished his term of office. His superiors decided to send him to Germany for six months to prepare for a doctorate. Bergoglio had chosen to work on the contribution of the Italian scholar Romano Guardini who had died in 1968.

A highly regarded philosopher and theologian, Guardini synthesized great liturgical thinkers of the past and applied their contribution to contemporary society. He was to have an influence on many of the theologians of the Second Vatican Council. By coincidence, Guardini was to be a great influence on Fr. Luigi Giussani, who became the founder of the influential religious group Communion and Liberation, of which Bergoglio was to become a passionate follower and whose books he read over several decades.

During his time in Germany Bergoglio saw a painting that greatly appealed to his imagination. The canvas by the eighteenth-century Bavarian artist Johann Georg Schmidtner hangs in the church of St. Peter am Perlach in Augsburg. It depicts the Blessed Virgin Mary untying knots in a cord, an image inspired by the writings of third-century writer St. Irenaeus of Lyons. It was a gift of Canon Hieronymus

Ambrosius Langenmantel whose grandparents prayed to Our Lady as they were contemplating separating from each other. Their prayers seemed to have been answered, and in thanksgiving their grandson commissioned this painting for a chapel in the church of St. Peter am Perlach. The image so appealed to Bergoglio that he asked a printer in Argentina to make a copy. It subsequently became enormously popular and, thanks to the efforts of Bergoglio, is venerated throughout Argentina and Brazil.

Six months at the Institute of Sankt Georg at Frankfurt proved inconclusive. Failing to choose a subject, Bergoglio returned home; he decided not to proceed with the doctorate.

On his return to Argentina in late 1986, Bergoglio was appointed by the new provincial, Fr. Victor Zorin, as confessor and spiritual director to the Colegio Del Salvador in Córdoba, a role he retained until 1990. In addition he taught one day a week at the Colegio Máximo. He also assisted as a confessor in the nearby Jesuit church. Once more, Bergoglio offered his services to the local parish, celebrating Mass, hearing confessions, and meeting the people of the district.

CHAPTER THREE

Bishop of Buenos Aires

The apostolic nuncio to Argentina, Archbishop Ubaldo Calabresi, whose lengthy tenure ran from 1981 to 2000, occasionally consulted Fr. Bergoglio with regard to candidates for the episcopacy. The Italian-born Calabresi, a native of Sezze Romano, held Bergoglio in high esteem and valued his comprehensive knowledge of the clergy of several dioceses. Most conversations were carried out by telephone but occasionally Bergoglio was summoned to discuss issues directly with the Vatican diplomat.

On one occasion, May 13, 1992, Archbishop Calabresi suggested that the two meet at the airport. It would suit the travel plans of both men. Taking the Jesuit aside, the nuncio spoke of several issues, asking Bergoglio's opinion. As the call was made over the loudspeaker for passengers to board the plane, the nuncio casually remarked, "Ah . . . one last thing . . . you've been named auxiliary bishop of Buenos Aires, and the appointment will be made official on the twentieth."[1]

Bergoglio was taken aback by this unexpected news. He recalled later that he literally froze, unable to answer.

Bergoglio accepted the task conferred by Pope John Paul II, for obedience to the pope is one of the hallmarks of the Jesuit Order.

Calabresi was not the instigator of the appointment. Cardinal Antonio Quarracino, archbishop of Buenos Aires, had six auxiliary bishops to assist him in administering the diocese. While most of the bishops were diocesan, Quarracino wanted Bergoglio to bring something of his experience of the consecrated life.

The episcopal ordination took place on June 27, 1992, in Buenos Aires Metropolitan Cathedral. Cardinal Quarracino was the principal consecrator, assisted by Archbishop Calabresi and Bishop Emilio Ogñénovich. The new bishop invited his brothers and sisters, along with other members of the family. A large number of Jesuits attended the ceremony of their former provincial. The province was still divided over Bergoglio's term of office.

Christianity came to Latin America at the end of the fifteenth century, following the commercial voyages made by European explorers. Conversion to Catholicism was rapid among those who came in contact with the European conquerors. The reasons were varied. While some converted by conviction, a large number were forcibly baptized by the Spanish and Portuguese friars who settled in the New World and founded missions. For many Europeans the Americas were a lucrative source of material for the slave trade.

During the early decades of colonial settlement, the church offered little criticism of the Spanish and Portuguese overlords who took advantage of the riches of the new countries. Many indeed cooperated with the massive exploitation of hundreds and thousands who were sold into slavery. Although there were significant exceptions, such as the efforts made by the

Dominican friar Bartolomé de las Casas, most church authorities tacitly colluded with the colonial powers. For some fifty years, de las Casas vigorously defended the rights of the indigenous population who were exploited by Spanish slave traders. Another Dominican friar, Francisco de Vitoria (1483–1546), also defended the rights of the indigenous Indians against the encroachments of Spanish slave traders.

The first traces of settlement in Buenos Aires date to the mid-sixteenth century when the Spanish explorers led by Pedro de Mendoza set up a village in 1536. This was abandoned five years later in 1541 and lay desolate until the Spanish conquistador Juan de Garay refounded the town in 1580. Henceforth it would be known as the town of the Most Holy Trinity and the Port of Holy Mary of the Fair Winds. As pope, Francis chose to visit the Shrine of Our Lady of the Fair Winds at Cagliari in Sardegna for one of his first pastoral visits. Gradually the city became an important port for Spanish traders.

The Diocese of Buenos Aires was formed on April 6, 1620, with the appointment of the first bishop, Fray Pedro Carranza (1621–1632). The new diocesan territory was divided from the nearby Diocese of Paraguay. A native of the Spanish city of Seville and a member of the Carmelite Order, Bishop Carranza encouraged clergy to come from Spain and work in the new diocese. The bishop recounted that the diocese numbered little more than one hundred houses, not including the population that worked on the plantations. With encouragement from the king of Spain, a number of clerics crossed the Atlantic to help the fledgling diocese.

In 1776 the Viceroyalty of the River Plate was established from that of Peru. This territory was the last of the districts loyal to the Spanish crown. By the early nineteenth century, the people of the viceroyalty sought independence from

Spain. Incursions by the British navy in 1806 led indirectly to the War of Independence.

In May 1810 the people of Buenos Aires rebelled against the Spanish authorities who administered the city. The Spanish monarch Ferdinand VII had been deposed two years earlier by Napoleon. In late 1810 Paraguay declared independence, and the following year King Ferdinand was restored to the throne. His immediate difficulties lay in securing his grasp of power in Spain; the colonies would have to await his consideration. During the interregnum and early months of the restoration of power, the locals attempted to establish their independence. On July 9, 1816, politicians met at Tucumán, some eight hundred miles north of Buenos Aires. Here they declared the independence of the United Provinces of South America from Spanish rule. On March 5, 1866, Buenos Aires was elevated to the status of an archdiocese, composed of parts of Paraná, La Plata, Montevideo, and Viedma.

In the intervening centuries the diocese was cared for by both Spanish and native Argentinian clergy. By the time of the election of Jorge Bergoglio to the papacy in 2013, the diocese had grown to an area of more than seventy-five square miles with a population of more than two and a half million Catholics.

The challenge of working as a bishop in this multicultural city was immense. As a native of the city, Bergoglio was aware of the inequality of the citizens. While some lived in considerable luxury there were enormous numbers whose lives were stunted by poverty. In a sign of solidarity with the poorer areas, Bergoglio gave his first interview as a bishop to a parish newsletter, *La Estrella de Belén*.

For administrative purposes the Diocese of Buenos Aires is divided into four zones, Flores, Devoto, Belgrano, and Centro, originally satellite towns that surround the city of

Buenos Aires. Bishop Bergoglio was immediately appointed episcopal vicar of the Flores district, where he had grown up. On December 21, 1993, he was also entrusted with the central office of vicar general of the archdiocese. The latter appointment showed how much Querricino had grown to trust the Jesuit in the short period since his appointment.

The modern city of Buenos Aires lies on the estuary of the de la Plata River and is one of the twenty largest cities in the world. The population of the greater Buenos Aires area comprises thirteen million people.

For the new bishop the challenge was to find a method of connecting people with the church. Decades of dictatorship had disillusioned thousands of Argentinians and many had lost faith in the church. During the various coups, the bishops had generally kept silent with regard to the rape, torture, and kidnapping in which thousands of citizens died. If his term as bishop was to be fruitful, the challenge lay in presenting the Christian faith in an attractive manner and also disassociating himself from the recent past.

Initially Bishop Bergoglio moved into a Jesuit house in Buenos Aires. Used to living in community for so much of his life, Bergoglio refused the spacious residence offered to him by the diocese close to the cathedral.

The experience was not universally harmonious. Some of his companions disliked having their former provincial living among them as a bishop. There was a suspicion among a few that, although now a diocesan bishop, he was still meddling in the internal affairs of the order. Many had not forgiven him for the divisions and hurts caused during his term of office as provincial. There were tensions in the house, and some felt that the bishop should leave.

Auxiliary bishops carry out the duties assigned to them by the archbishop but Bergoglio took the initiative to visit the district of which he was in charge. Rather than arrange formal meetings or visits to parishes, Bishop Bergoglio preferred to drop in unannounced. In particular he made a distinct effort to be available for clergy. Bergoglio's style was markedly different from previous bishops. He consulted and listened even if the responsibility for decisions ultimately lay with him.

The slum areas on the periphery were the first focus of his attention as he urged the wealthier parishes to dispose of some of their resources to help the needy parishes in the shantytowns where houses were made of brick, cardboard, and tin.

In 1990 Bergoglio had come into contact with a group of volunteers of Puntos Corazón, the "Heart's Home," a charitable organization founded by the French priest Thierry de Roucy. Bergoglio was impressed by the dedication of the workers who went to live in poor areas in order to help those living with difficulties. De Roucy encouraged the volunteers to be kind to the lonely and do whatever was possible to help them. De Roucy did not advocate building structures. He thought it was sufficient to visit people in their homes and offer simple but effective help and companionship. Bergoglio was impressed by the compassion of the volunteers, most of whom gave up more than a year of their lives to help people in difficulty in many countries throughout the world.

As bishop, Jorge Bergoglio needed to inspire both the diocesan clergy and the members of religious orders. He often claimed that his priests were his parish. If he looked after them, they would work well with and for the parishioners. With only 850 priests in an expanding diocese of 2.5 million Catholics, he needed to care for each one. He continuously encouraged them to look after their health and, when in difficulty, to come to him for help. In particular he kept in contact with the members of religious orders who helped administer a number of parishes, oratories, hospitals, and schools.

Not all priests were happy with this new style. Some resented Bergoglio's constant criticism of those who were not as dedicated to their ministry as he expected. On several occasions he urged priests not to drive the latest model car and to avoid luxury in dress and style of life.

Written correspondence was attended to as soon as was practical, although Bergoglio disliked desk work. In his pocket he carried a small notebook in which he noted down any requests or requirements to attend to when he returned home.

Although he established a good rapport with his priests, Bergoglio was also demanding. If he noted that one was not doing his fair share of pastoral work, he would let him know quite crisply. And Bergoglio was also fair, arranging for priests in difficulty to have counseling and offering financial support.

In an in-depth interview for *The Jesuit*, given to journalists Sergio Rubin and Francesca Ambrogetti in 2010, Cardinal Bergoglio recalled how a wise priest noted that most clergy are happy to have ninety-nine sheep in the fold and fail to go after the one missing. The task of the priest is to leave the pen in the care of others and search for the lost sheep. This was to become a leitmotif of his pontificate.

Bergoglio believed that good parish structures were important, but he often lamented that priests were too busy with administrative tasks that were not their expertise and should be attended to by competent people in the parish, especially with the declining practice rate in Argentina.

Cardinal Quarracino established a good working relationship with Bergoglio and spoke well of him. "I know where

Bishop Bergoglio is even if I don't see him," he joked at meetings of the bishops. Bergoglio was always in the last row. With his ready smile the new bishop sought to put people at ease. He insisted on being called *Father* rather than any greater ecclesiastical title.

Although entitled to a car, Bergoglio preferred to use public transport, preferably the bus or metropolitan underground. Usually people did not pay attention to him but it was an important way for him to keep in contact with his fellow citizens.

On June 3, 1997, Pope John Paul II appointed Bishop Bergoglio as coadjutor to the elderly Cardinal Quarracino. As his retirement approached, Cardinal Quarracino had flown to Rome to put pressure on the Congregation of Bishops to appoint Bergoglio with the right of succession. Although unable to obtain a private audience with Pope John Paul, Quarracino got a message through to the pontiff who acceded to the cardinal's request.

Eight months later, on February 28, 1998, Quarracino suffered a fatal heart attack and Bergoglio automatically became archbishop and metropolitan of Buenos Aires. Six months later on November 6, he was appointed by Pope John Paul II as the ordinary for the large population of Eastern Rite Catholics who lacked their own bishop. The following June, Archbishop Bergoglio traveled to Rome to receive the *pallium*, the role of office for metropolitans. The archbishop dissuaded most of his family and friends from attending.

As archbishop of Buenos Aires, Bergoglio was entitled to move into the grandiose official residence. Protesting that he had been used to living in one room since he entered the Jesuits, he continued to live in the small single-bedroom apartment close to the curial offices. This had been a retirement apartment for the elderly Bishop Ogñénovich, formerly custodian of the shrine of Our Lady of Luján. Living by himself he shopped in the local grocery store and cooked his own meals. He rarely went out at night either for dinner or events.

The furnishings of the apartment were sparse. The crucifix over his bed had been inherited from his grandparents Giovanni and Rosa. A picture of Mary, Joseph, and Jesus that had belonged to his family also hung on the wall. The small wardrobe contained the few dark clothes he wore. Once a week a woman came to do the laundry. The furnishings of the adjacent book-lined room were sparse. On the desk and bookshelves were several photographs sent by people he had met in the slums along with some family photographs. The studio opened into a small kitchen. At lunch the archbishop preferred to eat a light snack, avoiding luncheon invitations.

As bishop, Bergoglio maintained the habit of years in Jesuit communities. Each morning he rose before 5:00. The early hours of the morning were for prayer in his small chapel and study. While the day was full of appointments, visits, and activities, the evening was mostly reserved for his meal and a few phone calls to family and friends. For recreation he listened to the radio and retired early most evenings. On one occasion he received a gift of some CDs. Unsure what they were or how they worked, he later asked a friend to record them to cassettes, as he did not have a CD player.

When he became archbishop, Jorge Bergoglio installed a special phone line for the priests, giving them his confidential number. They knew that if they were in trouble or needed help in any manner they could call him. To ensure his availability he dedicated an hour each morning between 7:00 and 8:00 when he would answer the phone personally. There would be no intermediaries, and each request for advice or help would be dealt with immediately. The calls worked both ways because often Bergoglio took the initiative to make a call. While most were offers to help, Bergoglio also called priests asking for a report on their work.

In the diocesan offices, the archbishop had the assistance of secretaries and staff. The diocese runs several ministries for migrants, the poor, the sick, youths, and the elderly. These are delegated to a number of administrators, all of whom answer to the archbishop. Considering the large size of the diocese, Bergoglio was assisted by six auxiliary bishops and one priest secretary. The group met every two weeks in the diocesan offices and discussed the pastoral care of the people. Several times a year the archbishop met with the elected council of priests.

Shortly after he became archbishop, Jorge Bergoglio established a commission to examine the financial situation, following the arrest of Monsignor Roberto Toledo, the vicar general and former private secretary of Cardinal Quarracino. Other people were also questioned, including Juan Miguel Trusso, the son of a former Argentinian ambassador to the Holy See.

The arrest of Toledo by the financial police was connected to the failed Banco de Crédito Provincial and charges of corruption. The police had been alerted to irregularities and in December 1998 demanded to examine the archives of the deceased Cardinal Quarracino. On legal advice, Bergoglio countered by contesting that the Argentinian Central Bank had failed its duty in exposing investors in the Banco de Crédito Provincial. A court case was initiated to defend the church from unjust charges.

The report of the cardinal's commission recommended transferring diocesan accounts from local banks into the larger international banks such as HSBC and UBS, which would lessen the exposure of the diocese in the event of financial collapse. Bergoglio restructured the financial administration of the diocese, insisting on meticulous accountancy and transparency.

On February 21, 2001, Archbishop Bergoglio was created a cardinal in a consistory, which took place at the Vatican. Learning of his promotion, Bergoglio requested the many people who wanted to accompany him to the ceremony in Rome to remain at home and donate the money to the poor. When the Argentinian Embassy to the Holy See in Rome offered a dinner and reception for the new cardinal, Bergoglio declined at first but was finally persuaded when told that his refusal would cause offense to Argentinians in Rome.

As a Jesuit, Bergoglio had taken a vow never to seek high office in the church but now he had reached the second highest office. Bergoglio traveled with his sister María Elena to Rome with a small number of relatives and friends. María Elena recalled how the pair met another bishop who asked if Bergoglio had managed to get a car from the Vatican to transport them around the city. "It is all taken care of," replied the cardinal-elect. It was not quite true for they trudged on foot throughout the streets of Rome. "And," she added, "for him it was not easy, with his flat feet that always give him trouble."

On the morning he was to be created cardinal, Father Guillermo Marcó went to Casa del Clero close to Piazza Navona to meet the cardinal-elect. Marcó had assisted the archbishop unofficially since dealing with the media following the financial scandal of 1998. It was a wise move. Bergoglio could be dour in public while Marcó was popular with journalists. The two had agreed to meet and travel together to the Vatican, a little over a mile away.

When the cardinal emerged from the residence, Marcó looked around for the official car. "How are we traveling?" he asked politely.

"What do you mean?" came the reply. "We are going to walk."

The young cleric was slightly embarrassed as the two started off in the direction of the Vatican with Bergoglio dressed in bright scarlet robes. All the more so when they stopped in a bar for a coffee on the way. Seeing his companion's discomfort, Bergoglio laughed. "Don't worry! In Rome you can walk around with a banana on your head and nobody will notice!"

It is traditional to assign a titular church to each cardinal, recalling that the office of cardinalate was originally a parish pastor of Rome. Bergoglio was assigned to the Church of St. Robert Bellarmine in the fashionable Parioli district of Rome. The church bore the name of the famous sixteenth-century Jesuit archbishop and post-Tridentine theologian who in two conclaves had declined the papacy.

Bergoglio took advantage of the visit to Italy to retrace his roots in northern Italy. Traveling to Turin with his sister, the pair met some relatives in Portacomaro. The visit was private, and Jorge and María Elena went to see the house where their father had been born and grew up. Although it had been sold in 1929 the new owners showed the Argentinian visitors the house and property. Brother and sister walked arm in arm through the small fields, among the grapevines and olive trees. When he left, one of his relatives gave him a small bag. "This is some of your native soil," he said. "Take it back with you to Argentina and remember where you come from."

The attacks on the Twin Towers in New York and the Pentagon in Washington on September 11, 2001, caused reverberations throughout the world. Three hijacked planes crashed into buildings that killed both passengers aboard and several thousands working in the buildings. When a terrorist group, Al Qaeda, claimed responsibility for the attacks, America and her allies prepared an offensive to destroy them and their supporters.

At the Vatican preparations were underway for the Synod of Bishops. The assembly of senior bishops from all over the world takes place with the pope every two or three years. Established in 1965, the synod was one of the first fruits of the Second Vatican Council (1962–1965). The synod was designed as a means of allowing the bishops of the church to meet regularly and examine contemporary issues. Although not an executive body the issues discussed by the bishops reached a global audience. The theme of the assembly was "The Role of the Bishop in the Third Millennium." In reality it held little interest to most Catholics.

Cardinal Edward Egan, archbishop of New York, stayed in New York in the aftermath of the attack. In his place Pope John Paul appointed Cardinal Bergoglio as adjunct relator general, or chairman of the synod. Since Egan did not attend, the synod was effectively administered by Bergoglio. It was the Argentinian's debut on the international scene.

The synod took place during the first three weeks of October, and Bergoglio oversaw the daily sessions. The participants numbered 252 synodal bishops from 118 countries as well as a number of experts and observers.

Participants recall Bergoglio's stewardship of the synod as efficient and appreciated the speed with which he dispatched business. With good humor he was able to cut the speeches of long-winded bishops at the microphone. "We have to be home by Christmas," he occasionally joked in his low voice.

The synod gave Bergoglio the opportunity to meet most of the episcopal delegates and learn about their experiences in their home dioceses. As he listened to their aspirations and problems he formed a broader idea of the challenges facing bishops throughout the world. The bishops took notice of the soft-spoken prelate who patiently worked through the vast bureaucracy to bring the final report to the pope.

John Paul's pontificate was marked by a strong concern for social justice. During his apostolic journeys around the globe he readily criticized policies that he saw as contrary to God's plan. Bergoglio's concern in areas of social and ethical concern was less idealistic as a response to the concrete needs of people.

In 2001 Argentina experienced a dramatic economic crisis caused by a Russian and Mexican financial collapse in 1998. During general elections two years later the governor of Santa Cruz province, Néstor Kirchner, emerged as the victor when President Carlos Menem withdrew from the presidential race. However, in a low turnout of the electorate, Kirchner had gained only 22 percent of the votes. In his inauguration speech the president pledged to improve the declining economy and restore prosperity to the country.

Cardinal Bergoglio was vocally critical of both politicians and citizens who failed to protect the weak in society and regularly decried the lack of motivation to eradicate poverty. On the same day of the president's inauguration, the cardinal presided at the annual *Te Deum* celebration to mark National Independence Day. Developing the patriotic theme Bergoglio called for a just system that would care for the poorest people in the country, criticizing "the invisible dictatorship of those hidden interests which have taken over the resources and our capacity to evaluate and to think."

The new president interpreted the cardinal's words as a personal attack and declined to attend further such ceremonies. Bergoglio always had a strained relationship with politicians, especially those in government, and he never missed an opportunity to debate or to criticize. He was scathing of politicians who failed to improve the economy and social status of the people. Although he rarely issued press releases, he used homilies and sermons to deliver his message. Each year at the Chrism Mass of Holy Thursday he explained to the people and priests his plans for the coming months. These homilies were often read afterward by politicians who perceived Bergoglio as a force with which to be reckoned.

Bergoglio had a pragmatic approach to the administration of his diocese. In an interview with the journalist Stefania Falasca in 2007 for the Italian magazine *30 Giorni*, Cardinal Bergoglio expressed his no-nonsense approach to the people in the diocese. He had high standards for his clergy. Because the archbishop was a Jesuit and not a member of the diocesan presbyterate, it caused some friction between prelate and clerics. Bergoglio challenged the priests to work hard for the people. Rather than wait for them to come to the parish, the priests were to go to the people.

"In Buenos Aires," Bergoglio noted, "there are about two thousand meters [1.2 miles] between one parish and the next. So I said to the priests: 'If you can, rent a garage and, if you find some willing layman, let him go there! Let him be with those people a bit, do a little catechesis and even give Communion if they ask him.' A parish priest said to me: 'But Father, if we do this the people then won't come to church.' 'But why?' I asked him. 'Do they come to Mass now?' 'No,' he answered. And so! Coming out of oneself is also coming out from the fenced garden of one's own convictions, considered irremovable, if they risk becoming an obstacle, if they close the horizon that is also of God."[2]

Bergoglio could be severe with his priests, poking fun at the pomposity of some clergy. "I sometimes tell them to look at the peacock. He looks wonderful from the front with shining feathers. But then look at him as he passes from behind, and there you have a different story!"

In the late 1960s and 1970s, a number of priests in Buenos Aires began to work in the shantytowns on the outskirts of the city. According to July 2004 estimates, there were about 640 slums in these areas of suburban Buenos Aires. About 690,000 people lived in the crowded areas, packed into 111,000 makeshift dwellings. There was no sanitation, and open sewers lined the roads. In the summer the slums were scorching hot, and in the damp winter the shelters were regularly flooded.

In May 1968 several priests met together to discuss ways to support the poor people who lived in the *villas miserias*. This was the era of what is loosely called "liberation theology." A year earlier Pope Paul VI had published a milestone encyclical, *Populorum Progressio*, concerning the development of the world, its people, and natural resources. In the encyclical, the pope had stated: "No one may appropriate surplus goods solely for his own private use when others lack the bare necessities of life."[3] The pope had urged solidarity with the poor and challenged the political structures that allowed poverty to grow relentlessly.

With the tacit support of several bishops the priests set up a movement, *Movimiento de Sacerdotes para el Tercer Mundo*, Movement of Priests for the Third World. The aim of the clergy was to educate the illiterate and equip youth for employment. They had been inspired by a document that had appeared a year earlier, the "Manifesto of 18 Bishops of the Third World." This charter had challenged the abuse of political and economic power that deprived vast numbers of humanity their basic rights and dignity.

The first priests, numbering a dozen, received permission to work in the slums of Buenos Aires. Fired with enthusiasm they built simple chapels and fostered the people's devotion to the saints. They also attracted the attention of those who used the people of the district as drug pushers and other petty criminals.

The developments alarmed the government forces as the priests supported the workers' rights to strike and demand fair pay. The military dictatorship of General Juan Carlos Onganía prohibited these rights. The dictator announced that he would demolish the shantytowns if the people did not desist from political agitation. In December 1969 twenty priests marched on the government offices protesting against the plan. An auxiliary bishop of Buenos Aires, Juan Carlos Aramburo, threatened the priests with canonical sanctions unless they desisted from stirring up political unrest.

A year later, however, support for the clergy came from a number of bishops and fellow clerics. Many remained uneasy with the Leftist politics espoused by several of the more politically minded clergy. In July 1970 a seminal document was published, the "Declaration of Argentinian Priests." It stated: "We are a group of Argentinian priests who, despite our deficiencies, seek to love Jesus Christ, the Church and the Fatherland. We belong to that great part of the Church which seeks to promote the material and spiritual good of people, of the well-off and of the poor. However, we walk an entirely different path from that of Marx, Lenin, Che or Mao."

These were years of global unrest. Bolivia and Argentina were in the throes of political upheaval while war in Vietnam turned into a protracted strife in which the United States was engaged with disastrous results. Priests for the Third World, the movement of the Argentinian priests, demanded social change. Some even engaged in an armed struggle. The differences of opinion between members eventually led to the dissolution of the movement in 1976. Although as Jesuit provincial Bergoglio was skeptical of the aims of the priests, as archbishop of Buenos Aires he strongly supported the priests who volunteered to work in the villas. Although the number of vocations to the priesthood declined during his years as bishop, the number of priests working in the villas tripled. Even the newly ordained were encouraged to spend some part of their ministry among the poorest people of the diocese.

"It is not enough to visit the slums," he told a gathering of clergy. "We need priests to live with the people there as much as in our other parishes throughout Buenos Aires." At the same time he appointed some young priests to posts of responsibility for which they had not sufficient training, often with poor results.

From the number of candidates who presented themselves to enroll in the seminary each year, only 40 percent were chosen. Having spoken to a vocations director, the candidates were invited to spend weekends together before making a decision to study for the priesthood. For some the priesthood was not a suitable option. For others, the diocese was not the best choice, and the vocations director would guide them toward religious orders more in tune with their talents. The archbishop met with the vocations director regularly and attended some of the weekend seminars each year to encourage those thinking of entering the priesthood.

To show his practical support for the priests and the people of the villas, Bergoglio often turned up unannounced to administer baptisms or confirmations. Sometimes, where phones did not exist in the shantytowns, it was not possible to contact the priests in advance of a visit.

Outside Constitución Station, youths from the parish of Santa Elisa and those of the Virgen de Caacupé regularly helped the local clergy. Colorful banners, announcing baptisms and confessions, were hung from poles. The local people often approached the priest for a blessing. Amid the hustle and bustle of the marketplace, Mass was celebrated on the side of the street. Bergoglio, without any fuss, simply celebrated Mass and spoke in simple terms to those gathered around the portable altar.

The cardinal also showed his support for priests working in challenging circumstances. Whenever he heard of a priest who was sick or needed a break, he phoned him and offered to act as a substitute. The cardinal supported his priests when he knew they were in danger. During the dictatorship many priests and seminarians were abducted and tortured. At least eighteen priests were killed. In the first half of his period in office as provincial, Bergoglio had experienced the terror and shock of sudden attacks and murders of church personnel. When the military targeted priests, the bishops were not always vocal in their support.

On May 11, 1974, Fr. Carlos Mugica was assassinated outside the church of San Francisco Solano, in the district of Mataderos, while talking to a young couple about their forthcoming wedding. He was regarded as too close to the Perón faction.

The death of the priest shocked the people of the district who immediately saw him as a martyr. At Bergoglio's instigation in 1999 the remains of the priest were disinterred from the middle-class cemetery of Recolita, where Evita Perón is buried, and brought back to the parish where he had exercised his ministry. The cardinal celebrated Mass on the occasion and led the procession when the remains of the beloved priest were reburied at the Church of Christ the Worker.

In a prayer of reparation, the cardinal expressed the sorrow of the people: "The death of Father Carlos, for his actual killers, for those who planned his death, for the complicit silences of most of society and for the times that, as members of the Church, we did not have the courage to denounce his assassination, Lord have mercy."

Today the memory of the handsome, charismatic priest is still venerated by the people whom he motivated and inspired.

In the early morning of July 4, 1976, worshipers arriving for Mass in the church of San Patricio found the doors shut. The church, administered by the Pallotine Fathers, is in the middle-class suburb of Belgrano, in the north of Buenos Aires. A young man, the organist Rolando Savino, offered to climb in a window of the brown brick church. To his horror he found the bodies of five men lying in a pool of blood on the floor. On a door near the bodies, which lay face upward, was scrawled the words: *"Por los camaradas dinamitados en Seguridad Federal. Venceremos. Viva la Patria."* (For the comrades blown up at Federal Security. We will prevail. Long live the Fatherland.)

Close by, on the carpet, appeared the words: *"Estos zurdos murieron por ser adoctrinadores de mentes vírgenes y son M.S.T.M."* (These left-wingers were killed for being indoctrinators of innocent minds and M.S.T.M.)

The anagram referred to the movement of Priests for the Third World. The people were horrified as the doors were opened and the horror revealed. The three priests of the parish—Alfredo Leaden, 57, Alfredo Dufau, 67, and Alfredo

Kelly, 43—had been gunned down. Beside them lay the bodies of two seminarians, Salvador Barbeito, 29, who was rector of the local school, and Emilio Barletti, 23.

The massacre shocked the parish and the city. The military condemned the murder of the men, claiming that it was evidently the work of left-wing guerillas. Twenty police officers had been killed in a bomb explosion two days earlier. It may have been that the execution of the innocent clerics and students was a reprisal killing. In subsequent investigations it emerged that the military junta had authorized the killing. The papal nuncio, Archbishop Pio Laghi, who had arrived in Buenos Aires on April 27, 1974, was convinced that the military intended to subdue and intimidate church authorities with such acts of violence. In 1997 Bishop Bergoglio went to the parish to celebrate a Mass marking the anniversary of the massacre.

On July 4, 2001, the twenty-fifth anniversary of the killing, Cardinal Bergoglio returned to San Patricio to pray for the martyrs. Recalling the victims, he said: "I am a witness, because I accompanied Alfie in his spiritual direction, in his Confession, until his death. He only thought of God. And I name him because I am a witness to his heart, and when I mention him I mention all of them."

In August 2005 Cardinal Bergoglio gave permission to open the cause for beatification of the Pallotine victims. It was as much a political as a spiritual decision as the process will investigate the role of civil forces in the massacre. It also promises to stir up divisive memories for Catholics of the city.

At the end of a Mass celebrated in a *villa miseria* in 2009, the archbishop told the congregation that one of his priests had received a death threat. It brought back memories of the days of the military junta but now the assassins were drug barons, not soldiers.

The ever-present scourge of drug pushing and addiction was rampant in the slums. Along with some lay people, the parish priests in villa 21 had opened three centers for people who were trying to break their drug habit. This was the largest shantytown, with about fifty thousand people, among the twenty-four slums.

A young and idealistic priest who worked in villa 21, José María "Pepe" Di Paola, had been stopped by some men and told that he would be shot if he continued to assist the people at the center. Padre Pepe had opened a refuge in 2008 for young people, providing daily food and education as well as a social center for elderly people to meet.

In the past three decades Argentina, along with other Latin American countries, has been ravaged by the illegal drugs industry, in particular *paco*, a low-grade residue of cocaine left over from the purer drug exported abroad. The drug addicts become entirely disorientated and unable to function. For many, especially youths, the only refuge is the parish. Here education programs are developed and efforts are made to find employment for the young people in danger. Often the drug pushers target children to smuggle and sell drugs for them on the streets of the major cities.

An important part of the church's mission is carried out by catechists. Often volunteers, these catechists assist parents and priests in educating the young people. They organize regular meetings, teaching the children prayers and the Bible. Often they act as social workers, trying to help families weighed down by poverty and substance abuse.

When Cardinal Bergoglio visited the slums, he spent time with catechists, encouraging their efforts. Having celebrated Mass he remained with the parishioners afterward to share a meal. He insisted on waiting in line to receive his plate with the others and then sat where he found an empty seat and chatted with the person next to him. It was not unusual for Bergoglio to share a common straw to drink *mate*, a strong tea popular in Argentina.

Often he would hear of family members in prison and would take out his black notebook and jot down the names of the loved ones. Within days he would quietly visit the prisons, bringing the greetings of family to the detainees.

Each year in October, Bergoglio celebrated Mass in a sports stadium for the youth of the diocese. The Mass was lively with the participation of exuberant young singers and musicians. He preached a short, simple homily. He appointed appropriate priests and catechists to be with the youth and was available for photographs afterward.

A man given to spontaneous gesture, it was evident that this came from a genuine caring for people. He was willing to change church practice in order to challenge people's perceptions, for example, celebrating Mass in hospitals and nursing homes. As a Jesuit, Bergolgio was marked as an unimaginative conservative, as a bishop and archbishop he developed a progressive streak. He no longer saw the poor as recipients of charity but rather people who had a right to at least a basic standard of living. After celebrating the annual Mass of the Chrism on Holy Thursday with people and clergy in the morning at the cathedral, in the afternoon Cardinal Bergoglio celebrated the Mass of the Lord's Supper in a city hospital, hospice, nursing home, or prison. After the homily, he reenacted the ceremony of the washing of the feet. For him, the gesture brought the gospel accounts of the Last Supper to life. He washed and kissed the feet of prisoners, drug addicts, people living with HIV/AIDS, prostitutes, and other people living in humiliating situations. He also washed the feet of children and the elderly in the tin-roofed churches of the villas miserias. While he never carried money on his person, Bergoglio later instructed his secretary to send the families money.

In May 2007, Pope Benedict undertook a five-day trip to Brazil, the world's most populous nation. Central to his pastoral visit was the inauguration of the Fifth General Conference of the Bishops of Latin America and the Caribbean over which Cardinal Bergoglio, as president, had asked him to preside.

Speaking at the Marian shrine of Aparecida on May 13, the pontiff expressed his support for the work of the bishops who served the Catholics of the continent and islands, often in difficult circumstances. Underlying the papal message, however, was a concern for the spiritual hemorrhaging of many Catholics from the faith. Inroads made by Pentecostals and fundamentalist sects threatened the sacramental life of the church. The other Christian churches and sects offered an attractive alternative to a stagnant form of Catholicism that was evident in some countries.

Cardinal Bergoglio was one of a small number of bishops who actively engaged with the evangelicals and often attended prayer meetings and religious services. On one occasion he caused surprise among the evangelicals and consternation among his flock as he knelt in prayer and asked his fellow Christian leaders to pray over him. It was a gesture that he was to repeat at a gathering of evangelicals in Rome during the second year of his pontificate.

The number of Latin American Catholics at the end of the first decade of the twenty-first century was some 432 million worshipers, three-quarters of the entire population. Brazil, with 134 million worshipers, is the largest Catholic country in the region and in the world. Numbers declined dramatically from 92 percent of the population in 1970 to 68 percent in 2012. Mexico, with 96 million Catholics, represents the second-largest Catholic population, followed by Colombia with 38 million Catholics.

The Catholic population of Argentina is 31 million. The smallest of the Catholic nations are Chile and Ecuador, each with 12 million adherents. The entire region makes up about 42 percent of the world's Catholics, even if the practice rate is low.

The task of the continent's church leaders, in a postmissionary period, was to encourage the development of the lay faithful and indigenous vocations. As president of the Argentinian Episcopal Conference since 2005, Cardinal Bergoglio played a key part in preparing a dossier for Benedict to read prior to his visit to Latin America, and he also assisted in drafting the pontiff's speeches and homilies.

Several bishops were apprehensive of Benedict's visit. As Prefect for the Congregation for the Doctrine of the Faith from 1981 until his election as pontiff in 2005, Cardinal Joseph Ratzinger had shown little sympathy for the theology of liberation. As pope, Benedict lamented the increase of abortion on the continent and cautioned against the excesses of both capitalism and Marxism. He urged Catholics to remain faithful to their church rather than embrace the various new churches and sects emerging on the continent.

With so many natives of Buenos Aires claiming European ancestry, the city also boasted large communities of the established Christian churches. Bergoglio had a particular affinity for the Orthodox faith, especially appreciating the veneration of the Blessed Virgin Mary that is so important in Orthodoxy.

Bergoglio established close links with the Greek Orthodox Metropolitan, Tarasios, of Buenos Aires and South America and regularly visited the archbishop and attended church ceremonies. On some occasions, he would attend simply dressed in his coat and stand at the back of the church with the people as the Divine Liturgy was celebrated in the sanctuary.

When Pope Benedict issued a document allowing Anglican converts to Catholicism to form a personal prelature, thus preserving elements of Anglican worship, Bergoglio expressed his exasperation. Speaking with Bishop Gregory Venables, former Anglican Primate in Argentina, he dismissed as unhelpful the pope's gesture in establishing an independent Ordinariate. Although he supported Christian unity, Bergoglio did not interpret this as the best method.

Bergoglio established a close relationship with the Jewish community of Buenos Aires, the largest in Latin America. The community had swollen during the period of the Second World War as thousands of German, Polish, and Russian Jews sought refuge in South America.

In the early 2000s the archbishop joined a Jewish-Catholic charitable organization called *Tzedaka* to help overcome poverty. With Jewish leaders he often visited the poor districts where Jewish people lived and offered his solidarity. Eleven years after the bombing of the Argentine Israeli Mutual Aid Center in which eighty-five people were killed and three hundred were injured, Bergoglio was the first signatory for a petition to bring the perpetrators to justice and rebuild the complex, which he later visited when it was completed. In July 2014 on the twentieth anniversary of the atrocity, Pope Francis sent a video message of solidarity, concluding, "along with my prayers for all the victims comes my desire for justice. May justice be done!"

In 2007 the cardinal attended a service to celebrate Rosh Hashanah at Benei Tikva Slijot synagogue and offered good wishes for the Jewish New Year. Having established good relations with his friend Rabbi Abraham Skorka, the two wrote a book, published in 2010 under the title *On Heaven and Earth*. The two men continued to broadcast a weekly program on the archdiocesan television station. Cardinal Bergoglio welcomed the opportunity to discuss interfaith relations, noting that "we succumb as victims of attitudes that don't permit us to have dialogue: arrogance, not knowing how to listen, hostility in our speech, attacking the messenger and so many others. Dialogue is born from an attitude of respect toward the other person, from a conviction that the other has something good to say."

Some years later, in December 2012, the cardinal attended the Hanukkah ceremony held in the Temple NCI-Emanu El in Buenos Aires. As a tribute to his steadfast support and friendship with the community in the city, he was invited to light the first flame on the menorah, the seven-branch candlestick.

Cardinal Bergoglio also fostered relations between Catholics and other faiths. During a visit to Germany in September 2006, Pope Benedict XVI gave a speech at Regensburg University. Many Muslims were offended by a citation concerning the Prophet Muhammad. In the verbal melee that ensued, relations between the Holy See and some Muslim authorities were strained. Bergoglio allowed a service to take place in the cathedral, in which Muslims and Catholics prayed that the difficulties could be resolved. In order not to offend Pope Benedict he did not attend.

As he built up relationships with the Muslim community in Buenos Aires, Bergoglio visited the At-Tauhid Mosque located in the neighborhood of Flores and the Arab–Argentine Ali Ibn Abi Talib School. On several occasions he was a guest of the Islamic Center of the Republic of Argentina and regularly invited religious representatives to dinner at the archbishop's residence. These were some of the rare occasions when he entertained guests. In November 2012, Muslims, Jews, and Christians prayed together in the cathedral. He was criticized for this by many who opposed common prayer of Christians and non-Christians in churches.

Cardinal Bergoglio was critical of unjust economic structures that create great inequalities. Speaking in 2009 he claimed that "unfair social debt is immoral, unjust, and illegitimate." Argentina was not exempt from criticism, and he urged everyone "to work to change the structural causes and personal or corporate attitudes that give rise to this situation (of poverty), and through dialogue reach agreements that allow us to transform this painful reality we refer to when we speak about social debt."

For that reason he urged political bodies, financial institutions, industries, trade unions, churches, and various charitable and social institutions to cooperate to help poor people free themselves from the barriers to charity.

During the early years of the third millennium, the state's attitude toward many ethical questions changed radically. In 1994 President Carlos Menem had declared his opposition to legalized abortion and instituted an annual Day for Life to be held on March 25. When Néstor Kirchner took office in 2003 government policies were modified. According to a survey published in 2007 by the Ministry of Health, the number of abortions each year ranged from 460,000 to 615,000. The president determined to introduce legislation surrounding the practice.

The bishops of the country vehemently opposed the proposal, and in 2007 the bishops of Latin America and the Caribbean published a document on the issue of abortion. Speaking at the launch of the document on October 2 of that year, Cardinal Bergoglio lamented the low value placed on human life. "The Church," he asserted, "is very conscious of the fact that the cheapest thing in Latin America, the thing with the lowest price, is life."

Bergoglio was pragmatic about sex education aimed at the appropriate age groups. The key to such formation, he argued, is respect for the human person aimed at the "age and receptivity of the young people."

The cardinal continued to oppose abortion and urged women to carry their pregnancies to term. In a speech in 2012 he asserted that "abortion is never a solution. We listen, support and offer understanding from our place to save two lives: respect the human being small and helpless, they (doctors) can take steps to preserve your life, allow birth and then be creative in the search for ways to bring it to its full development."

Cardinal Bergoglio was openly critical of some priests who refused to baptize children of unmarried parents. "In our ecclesiastical region there are priests who don't baptize the children of single mothers because they weren't conceived in the sanctity of marriage. These are today's hypocrites! Those who clericalize the Church. Those who separate the people of God from salvation. And this poor girl who, rather than returning the child to sender, had the courage to carry it into the world, must wander from parish to parish so that it's baptized!"

On another occasion, in an interview with the journalist Gianni Valente in the magazine *30 Days*, Cardinal Bergoglio recalled how he had met a woman during a visit to a parish to celebrate the feast of San Cayetano. She told him that she had seven children with two different fathers. Working as a maid, she did not have enough money to pay for a party or to invite all fourteen godparents to celebrate the christening.

The cardinal suggested a solution. If she was worried she could not gather all fourteen godparents together she could ask just two to represent the others. He invited her to bring the godparents and children to the chapel at his residence where he baptized all seven. After the private ceremony where the children were baptized, the cardinal provided refreshments, sandwiches, cakes, and soft drinks for the guests. When she was leaving, the mother thanked him for making her feel special, to which he replied, "Señora, where do I come in? It is Jesus who makes you important."

As archbishop of one of Latin America's premier cities, Bergoglio's words were listened to with special interest. He generally avoided giving interviews. "It's not my strong point," he insisted to journalists who constantly requested his comment on various subjects. Although shrewd he was wary of the pitfalls involved in granting interviews. His major interview, later published as *El Jesuita*, was given to two journalists who had gained his trust. Reserved by nature, Bergoglio nonetheless revealed his sense of humor, wit, sarcasm, determination, and depth of conviction.

Bergoglio was keenly aware of the importance of the media and became more so following his election to the papacy. His friendship with Rabbi Skorka and the conversations with him were unique in Latin America. The two hosted a weekly television show and also coauthored a book. The dialogue between the Jewish and Christian leaders provided an opportunity for each to explain to the other the intricacies of their respective faiths. They built up mutual trust and thus were able to pose difficult questions to each other.

The rule of celibacy for Latin-rite priests is a constant source of discussion and debate. Recalling a period as a seminarian when he developed a liking for a girl he met at an uncle's wedding, Bergoglio confessed that he was confused. Should he leave his religious vocation and follow her? He realized that such thoughts were entirely normal. For a long time, he told Rabbi Skorka, he struggled with the desire to leave and explore a relationship with the girl or remain in the seminary. After much soul searching he resolved to pursue his studies for the priesthood.

Bergoglio underlined his preference for celibacy but agreed that it was a theme in need of discussion. If the law of celibacy is relaxed, Bergoglio believed, it would be done on a regional basis, according to cultural demands, rather than a universal abolition of the requirement. This view of gradualness is a hallmark of his intellectual makeup that has also made him a formidable negotiator. On several occasions since his election to the papacy, Francis has expressed a willingness to reexamine the question of compulsory celibacy for diocesan priests.

Bergoglio did not talk about celibacy in a vacuum. Apart from his personal experience he dealt with many priests and even a bishop who broke their vows. In particular he was unique among the country's bishops in the kindness he showed toward a bishop who had resigned from his diocese and married, such as the case with Podestá.

Jerónimo Podestá, born in 1920, was a native of Ramos Mejía, close to the district of Buenos Aires where the Bergoglio family had settled. In 1962 he was consecrated a bishop and appointed to head the nearby diocese of Avellaneda-Lanús. He participated in the three sessions of the Second Vatican Council and was enthused by the discussions and debates in Rome. Podestá had a charismatic personality and worked to improve the conditions of the poor in his diocese.

On his return from the council in the mid-1960s Podestá fell in love with his secretary, Clelia Luro, a married mother of six children. The nuncio, Archbishop Umberto Mozzioni heard of the affair and requested Podestá to end it or resign as bishop. Podestá wavered between his vocation and his love for Clelia Luro and was forced to resign. The unprecedented marriage caused scandal in Argentina in 1972 when Podestá was laicized and married Luro. Two years later, the former bishop was exiled by the Alianza Anticomunista Argentina, the right-wing party, which found his politically progressive views unacceptable.

Podestá and his wife settled briefly in several cities: Paris, Mexico City, Rome, and also cities in Peru before he was allowed to return to Argentina when the dictatorship collapsed in 1983. By now, Podestá was largely forgotten. The scandal of the era had passed, and both he and Clelia lived in penury with no church pension to support them.

Clelia publicly acknowledged the kindness and attention she and her husband received from Bergoglio. When Podestá died, his widow wrote to Bergoglio, and continued to write on a weekly basis. As soon as he received the letter he phoned her to see how she was. After Podestá's death, Bergoglio was the only one to offer public support to her, and he also arranged for financial assistance. Even as pope he called each Sunday afternoon the octogenarian who had become a close friend.

While he was the first bishop to regularly visit the slum areas of his diocese, Bergoglio was attentive to all the parishes, accepting invitations to celebrate the sacraments and join in the life of the parish. When visiting parishes he always celebrated Mass with the people. Whether a beautiful church in a prosperous part of the city or in a poorer area where a church building did not exist, Bergoglio was happy simply to meet the people of the district.

He developed an easy style of preaching and encouraged people with anecdotes that evoked an emotional response. "I am a beggar," he often remarked. "I have to beg a lot of things from God. But I like to beg!" He rarely prepared texts, preferring to extemporize. People became used to his informality, his raised eyebrows, his laughs, and his intense sincerity.

However, Archbishop Bergoglio had to deal with sensitive issues that pertained both to the church in Argentina and the global church. As cases of cover-up of scandals were exposed in religious orders and dioceses throughout the world, Bergoglio was resolute in his views. In his conversations with Rabbi Skorka, Bergoglio addressed the issue of pedophilia. Although he claimed not to have had first-hand experience of instances of pedophilia, he recounted how an American bishop had once asked him for advice. The cardinal was clear:

> I told him to take away the priests' faculties, not to permit him to exercise his priestly ministry again, and to initiate a canonical trial in the tribunal that corresponds to that diocese. . . . I do not believe in the positions that some hold about sustaining a certain corporate spirit so as to avoid damaging the image of the institution. That solution, I believe, was proposed at some point in the United States: to move priests from one parish to another. That is stupid because, in that way, the priest carries his baggage with him. The corporate reaction carries such a consequence, and because of that I do not believe in these ways out. Recently, in Ireland, they uncovered cases that occurred for twenty years, and [Benedict XVI] clearly said: "Zero tolerance with this crime." I admire the courage and the straightforwardness of Benedict XVI on this point.[4]

Shortly before he concluded his six-year term of office in 2011 as president of the Episcopal Conference of Latin America and the Caribbean, Bergoglio led the bishops of Argentina in a public apology for the supine role some of their colleagues had taken during the Dirty War. Already on

April 27, 1996, the Argentinian bishops had issued an oblique apology for "sons of the Church which responded illegally to the guerrillas in a shocking and atrocious way, which brings shame to all." In 2010 Bergoglio spearheaded a more focused and honest admission that some bishops had failed to stop the massacres carried out by members of the military dictatorship. In some cases their deliberate silence contributed to the tortures and killings.

Another political clash came that same year as the government proposed legalizing same-sex marriages. The bishops opposed the intended legislation, arguing that it would change the whole nature and definition of marriage itself. In a letter dated July 8, 2010, to the Carmelite Sisters of Buenos Aires, Cardinal Bergoglio observed: "It is not a simple political struggle but pretends to destroy God's plan. It is not about a mere bill (this is only the instrument) but a move by the Father of Lies that seeks to confuse and deceive the children of God." However, while Bergoglio opposed the redefinition of marriage between two people of the same gender, he pragmatically acknowledged that civil provision was necessary.

Two weeks later on July 22, Argentina became the first country in Latin America to introduce the concept of same-sex marriage.

CHAPTER FOUR

The First Conclave

On the evening of April 2, 2005, Archbishop Leonardo Sandri announced to the tens of thousands gathered in St. Peter's Square that Pope John Paul II had died.

Karol Wojtyla had been elected on October 16, 1978, following the sudden death of Pope John Paul I after one month in office. The cardinal had been archbishop of Krakow, Poland, since January 1964. The cardinals gathered for that October conclave had been shaken by the unexpected demise of the pontiff. Spurred on to elect a younger and more robust pope, the cardinals chose the first non-Italian in five centuries. Taking the name John Paul in honor of his predecessor, the fifty-eight-year-old pope swept onto the world stage with an actor's flair and an athlete's energy. During a pontificate that lasted almost twenty-seven years he won both adoring fans and implacable critics.

As a youth, Wojtyla had lived through the horrors of the Second World War that had engulfed Europe between 1939 and 1945. His country of Poland had been invaded by both German and Russian troops. Human misery never before experienced on such a savage scale virtually destroyed the heartland of Europe.

When the war ended in 1945, a period of further stagnation and despair followed. Poland was brought into the orbit of Russian Communism and yet it did not lose its fierce nationalism that for centuries had been its proud hallmark. Wojtyla had tried to keep the Christian faith of his people alive during the atheistic Communist rule. He clashed regularly with the national authorities and argued for the freedom of worship for his people. As pope, he brought the same pugnacious style to his pontificate. Surviving an assassination attempt in 1981, John Paul saw his pontificate unfurl in a mystical manner.

John Paul took advantage of improved means of travel to bring the Gospel message to local churches. As he expounded doctrine to far-flung audiences he also centralized the church around Rome. While John Paul won popular appeal particularly through a series of 104 international visits, he also evoked fierce opposition to some of his uncompromising teachings on sexual mores and church discipline. John Paul was criticized for his authoritarian manner, his overly centralized government, women's role in the church, and the appointment of conservatives to the episcopate. While he was widely feted, much of his moral teaching was largely ignored. Ultimately an enigmatic figure, Pope John Paul II had expanded the profile of the papacy enormously.

More than one million mourners filed past the pontiff's corpse as it lay in state in St. Peter's Basilica. His funeral, the largest in history, was watched on television and the internet by a global audience of close to two billion people. The Patriarch of Constantinople, Bartholomew, attended the papal funeral, the first time such an event had occurred in the history of Christianity. The outpouring of grief was accompanied by calls from some quarters for him to be canonized immediately.

Owing to the lengthy pontificate the cardinals were faced with the dilemma of finding a pope to follow in the shadow of the late pontiff. Nobody could deny his inspiring sanctity, and the cardinals searched anxiously among their number.

In the early centuries the people and clergy of Rome elected their own bishop. During the ninth and tenth centuries the papacy was in the hands of a few powerful Roman families. To have a member a cardinal ensured the family's fortunes. In 1059, partly to avoid family factions, the election of a new pope was confined to the College of Cardinals. The assent of the clergy and people was given only after the election. In 1274 the concept of locking the cardinals into a hall was introduced to speed up the process. This followed a papal election at Viterbo that had lasted from November 1268 until September 1272.

In recent centuries, the papacy has become an office dreaded by most, desired by few. Expectations are high, and the stamina and dedication required appears at times to be beyond human capabilities.

While some argued for a return to the practice of the early church, with a body of electors made up of men and women of various nationalities and attributes, Pope John Paul II had left specific instructions on how the conclave should elect a new pope. All the cardinals were to assemble at the Vatican between fifteen and twenty days following the pontiff's death to meet in a series of General Congregations. A maximum of 120 of the cardinals under the age of eighty were to select the new pontiff by ballot. Confined to the Sistine Chapel for a series of votes each morning and afternoon, the election was to proceed until one candidate received a simple majority.

On April 18, 2005, the cardinals and the people of the city of Rome celebrated Mass at St. Peter's Basilica. Cardinal

Dean Joseph Ratzinger was the principal celebrant and delivered a short, analytical homily. Surveying the state of the church at the beginning of the third millennium, he noted how the barque of Peter seemed continuously buffeted by the winds of change. Noting the various ideologies that developed during the twentieth century, he observed, "Today, having a clear faith based on the Creed of the Church is often labeled as fundamentalism. Whereas relativism, that is, letting oneself be 'tossed here and there, carried about by every wind of doctrine,' seems the only attitude that can cope with modern times. We are building a dictatorship of relativism that does not recognize anything as definitive and whose ultimate goal consists solely of one's own ego and desires."[1]

That afternoon the 115 cardinal electors filed into the Sistine Chapel. Ratzinger's words had struck a deep chord with many. Placing his right hand on a copy of the Gospel, each cardinal swore in conscience to elect the one most suitable as successor to Peter. The cardinals who entered the conclave came from fifty countries; all but three had been created during John Paul's pontificate, the largest number in history to elect a pope.

The first ballot was taken that evening. Although inconclusive, it provided the cardinals with a small number of names from which the new pontiff would be chosen. The ballots were burned in a stove at the rear of the chapel. The cardinals had failed to identify a single candidate. A chemical powder was added to the paper ballots to produce a black smoke. When the burning ballot smoke emerged at 8:04 p.m. through a chimney in the roof visible from St. Peter's Square, the crowds gathered below knew that the ballots had been inconclusive.

The cardinals knew that it would be impossible to find a candidate who had attracted global attention with the success of John Paul II. The cardinals were anxious not to prolong the conclave as this would indicate division to the waiting world. The immediate requirement in the minds of most cardinals was continuity.

Although the cardinals were sworn to secrecy and had decided not to speak with the media until the conclave was over, the results of the balloting subsequently became broadly known. A cardinal kept a diary during the two-day conclave and the contents eventually leaked to the Italian press. According to the anonymous cardinal, Cardinal Joseph Ratzinger gained the most votes, followed at a distance by Cardinal Jorge Bergoglio and Cardinal Carlo Martini, the Jesuit archbishop of Milan. The latter explained that he suffered from Parkinson's disease and would not be a suitable candidate.

On the morning of April 19 the cardinals met once more in the chapel. The results of the two morning ballots were also inconclusive, but it was clear that Cardinal Ratzinger was approaching a majority. Bergoglio's votes were the next single block, probably numbering at least forty ballots.

At the first ballot of the afternoon session, Cardinal Ratzinger passed the required seventy-seven votes, obtaining the necessary two-thirds majority for a valid election. As the ballots continued to be counted, applause broke out throughout the chapel. The choice of the European indicated that the cardinals were not yet ready to consider a break from the Old World. Taking the name "Benedict," the new pope presented himself to the crowds in St. Peter's Square, explaining that he was "a humble worker in the vineyard of the Lord." His brief introduction ended with the blessing *urbi et orbi,* to the city and to the world.

CHAPTER FIVE

The Benedict Years

Unlike the unknown Wojtyla, Joseph Ratzinger was a familiar, if controversial, figure in the Vatican. A former professor of theology in several German universities and a prolific author, Joseph Ratzinger had been consecrated archbishop of Munich on May 28, 1977, and created a cardinal a month later. Following a papal visit to Germany in 1980, Pope John Paul II named Ratzinger Prefect of the Congregation for the Doctrine of the Faith on November 25, 1981. The Vatican would be home for the rest of his life.

As a theologian, Ratzinger had participated as a *peritus* or expert at the Second Vatican Council. He was seen as progressive and sought change in areas such as obligatory celibacy for the clergy. As Prefect of the Congregation for the Doctrine of the Faith, he took a strict approach to theologians whom he interpreted as liberal or unfaithful to the teaching of the church. During his period in office he played a pivotal role in the production of the General Catechism of the Catholic Church and a revision of the Code of Canon Law. In 2000 his office also issued a controversial document, *Dominus Iesus,* On the Unicity and Salvific Universality of

Jesus Christ and the Church. Although he had turned seventy-eight two days before his election, he set about following in the footsteps of John Paul II. Among his first acts was to approve the beatification process of his predecessor whom he beatified on May 1, 2011, and whose canonization he attended on April 27, 2014.

Benedict's love of theology and the liturgy permeated his pontificate. His homilies and catechesis were profound, and during his pontificate he produced a trilogy on the life of Christ. He generally followed the program laid out by John Paul II. An initial attempt to reform the Roman Curia was abandoned the year after his election. On July 7, 2007, he allowed the widespread use of the Latin liturgy that had been in use prior to the reforms introduced in the post-Vatican II era. It was an unsuccessful attempt to heal the rift between traditionalists attached to the old rite and mainstream Catholics. His lifting of a bar of excommunication on four bishops was severely criticized when one of them, Richard Williamson, controversially denied the horrors of the holocaust of Nazi Germany.

Benedict tried to strengthen the relationship introduced by Pope John XXIII between the Catholic Church and the Jewish faith. Relations with Islam faltered in 2006 when Pope Benedict quoted from an obscure medieval text that declared that the Prophet Mohammed, founder of the Islamic faith, was "evil and inhuman."' He was delivering a magisterial address at the University of Regensburg, where he had taught theology as a professor. The quotation from a fourteenth-century document was not understood by Muslims who reacted against the reports of the pontiff's remarks. Realizing the negative impact of his words, Benedict attempted to rectify the damaged relationships by inviting prominent Muslim clerics and leaders to meet him at Castelgandolfo. Benedict apologized for the misunderstanding while accepting that the quotation was misguided.

Pope Benedict had to deal with cases of clerical abuse, most of which had taken place prior to his election. The offenses were compounded by bishops and superiors who had willfully perverted the cause of justice by not denouncing clerics for their criminal actions to the civil authorities. In a strongly worded letter to the people of Ireland, Pope Benedict expressed his horror and revulsion while pledging to assist those who sought to overcome the emotional scarring caused by abuse. Both at the Vatican and on pastoral visits he met victims of the clerical abuse and offered comfort. Victims and their support groups were generally unimpressed by these gestures and called for the dismissal of bishops and superiors. These calls were routinely ignored by the Holy See.

In May 2012, *His Holiness* was published. This book by the Italian investigative journalist Gianluigi Nuzzi was based on letters and documents stolen from the desks of Pope Benedict and his private secretaries in the papal apartments. Although the journalist protected the thief of the documents, the pope's private secretary, Monsignor Georg Gaenswein, recognized a letter that could only be traced to the innermost circle at the private apartment. Calling together the immediate staff, the pope's butler and four women who cared for the papal apartment, Gaenswein confronted them with proof that one of them had stolen the documents. Although all denied it, Gaenswein handed the case to the Vatican's internal police. Following a raid on the apartment of the papal butler, some one thousand documents were found neatly stored in a set of cardboard boxes.

Paolo Gabriele, the forty-six-year-old butler, was placed on trial and convicted of larceny. Nuzzi indicated that there were several people involved in stealing the documents, including prelates who were clearly disloyal to the pope. For Gabriele, there were also the embarrassing questions of a gold nugget, a check made out to Pope Benedict, and a valuable antiquarian book that had also been taken from the papal apartment.

Among the most damning letters reproduced in the book was a letter from the irate future nuncio to the United States. Writing to Pope Benedict, Bishop Carlo Maria Vigano denounced the clientelism and dishonesty of many working within Vatican City State. It was evident that a dramatic rift had opened between Vigano and Cardinal Tarcisio Bertone, secretary of state. Benedict was forced to take sides. To Vigano's surprise, Benedict transferred him as apostolic nuncio to the United States of America. It was a classic case of *promoveatur ut moveatur*—promoted to get him out.

International interest was immediate. Media sources saw the events as further proof that the seat of administration for the global population of 1.2 billion people was at best in disarray and at worst corrupt. The pressure on the elderly pontiff was immense. Pope Benedict had begun to consider retirement in March 2012, following an exhausting visit to Mexico during which he suffered a fall at his residence. More recently he had received a heart pacemaker. As he faced a frail old age and increasing health worries he reluctantly took the decision to abdicate, the first reigning pontiff in almost six centuries to retire. Since in law nobody could accept his resignation, he chose the moment when he could announce his abdication to the assembled cardinals.

Shortly before his birthday, December 17, 2011, Cardinal Jorge Bergoglio submitted his resignation from office to Pope Benedict. The Code of Canon Law requires that diocesan bishops retire at the age of seventy-five. For bishops who are cardinals, retirement is often delayed for a year or two.

Bergoglio had made adequate preparations; his papers were in order and he had begun to donate his books to the seminary library. For his retirement, the archbishop intended to live in the diocesan home for priests, which was in his native district of Flores. He booked a room at the home and told the vicar general that he would be happy to assist in local parishes.

Bergoglio waited patiently for his resignation to be accepted but friends and colleagues noted that the cardinal did not seem anxious to retire. Several noted that he was morose when he spoke of life in retirement.

CHAPTER SIX

The Abdication

On the morning of February 11, 2013, Pope Benedict XVI met with cardinals resident in Rome for a public consistory in the Apostolic Palace at the Vatican. The occasion was to proclaim the canonization of a number of saints and to set the date for the public ceremony. Since it is a minor ritual, cardinals from outside Rome rarely traveled to take part. The pope, vested in a burgundy velvet cape and brocaded stole over his shoulders, sat on a gilt throne. The scarlet-vested cardinals were seated around the three walls of the Consistory Hall that were decorated with Renaissance tapestries. Shortly before the ceremony concluded, the pontiff added a few words in Latin, which, he noted, would be important for the life of the church. This was an understatement.

"After having repeatedly examined my conscience before God," Benedict said in a low voice, "I have come to the certainty that my strengths, due to an advanced age, are no longer suited to an adequate exercise of the Petrine ministry." Several of the cardinals present failed to understand the significance of the words delivered by the pontiff in Latin. Surprised glances were exchanged as the Latin words were slowly interpreted in whispers.

The pontiff explained the decline in mental and physical strength that he had experienced in recent months. "For this reason," he declared, "and well aware of the seriousness of this act, with full freedom I declare that I renounce the ministry of Bishop of Rome, Successor of St. Peter, entrusted to me by the cardinals on April 19, 2005, in such a way that as from February 28, 2013, at 8:00 p.m., the See of Rome, the See of St. Peter, will be vacant and a conclave to elect the new Supreme Pontiff will have to be convoked."[1]

The cardinals met the unexpected announcement with surprise and perplexity. None could have foreseen the pontiff's dramatic decision. Not since 1415 had a pontiff resigned. When Pope Gregory XII renounced the papacy, it was in the full flood of the Great Western Schism, a period in which three popes vied for validity. In order to allow a new pope to be elected the three had been forced to abdicate.

What Benedict would do in retirement was the subject of enormous speculation. Would he return to his native Bavaria or live in the seminary of Bressanone, where he had spent several holidays as cardinal? Would he retire to an Italian monastery, such as the famous abbey of Montecassino?

The pope chose to reside at the former gardener's house in the Vatican gardens. A community of contemplative nuns had lived and prayed in the converted house since 1994 when they were invited to live there by Pope John Paul II. The nuns had left the previous October and thus the property would be converted into a suitable residence for the retired bishop of Rome.

Hearing the news of Benedict's imminent departure, the remaining cardinals prepared to travel to Rome. On February 27, following a thirteen-hour flight, Cardinal Bergoglio arrived from Buenos Aires at Rome's Fiumicino Airport. Two other cardinals had arrived at the same time. Brazilian

Cláudio Hummes, former archbishop of Sao Paolo, was a Franciscan and had served for six years as Prefect for the Congregation for the Clergy. The two greeted each other with an embrace. "Who would have thought it?" asked Bergoglio rhetorically. Cardinal Luis Antonio Tagle of the Philippines was also awaiting his luggage. The two older men offered their congratulations to Tagle who had been named a cardinal the previous November. The cardinals had come to assist at a farewell audience given by Pope Benedict on the final morning of his pontificate.

The next morning the cardinals assembled in the Apostolic Palace to formally bid farewell to Benedict on his last day in office. Speaking in the Clementine Hall of the palace, Benedict XVI made his last official speech. It was a fitting end. His first official speech had been in the Sistine Chapel, celebrated with the cardinals following his election in 2005. Now, his last words were to the cardinals who would soon gather to elect his successor.

Assuring the cardinals that he would be close to them over the coming days he prayed that they would be completely docile to the action of the Holy Spirit in the election of the new pope. More important, he added, that he would also submit to the authority of a new pontiff, whomsoever it should be: "May the Lord show you the one whom he wants. And among you, in the College of Cardinals, there is also the future pope to whom today I promise my unconditional reverence and obedience."

In order to leave the cardinals entirely free from papal interference Pope Benedict had decided to withdraw to Castelgandolfo until the former convent had been converted. Shortly before 5:00 p.m. that afternoon Pope Benedict left the papal apartments that he had occupied for just less than eight years. As he exited from the elevator he took his cane in order to steady himself as he walked the final few paces to the courtyard of St. Damasus. His secretary and recently appointed prefect of the Papal Household, Archbishop Georg Gaenswein, stood behind him, his eyes moist with tears. The vicar of Rome, Cardinal Agostino Vallini, accompanied the pope as he saluted his staff for the last time.

As Benedict left the palace, applause fluttered about the small crowd of Vatican personnel that had gained access to the courtyard. The pope stepped into a black Mercedes for the short journey to the heliport that was designed in 1976 to allow the pope to leave and enter the Vatican without disrupting Roman traffic. At the heliport Cardinal Angelo Sodano, dean of the Sacred College, saluted Benedict as he prepared to leave the Vatican for the last time as pope.

The white helicopter rose into the sky and circled St. Peter's Square before veering out over the Tiber River. People had crowded into the piazza to watch the historic spectacle as the bells tolled from St. Peter's Basilica. On the roof of the North American College overlooking St. Peter's, Cardinal Timothy Dolan led the seminarians in their last salute. The journey lasted barely fifteen minutes as the helicopter flew south toward the Alban Hills. The sun had almost set as the helicopter landed on the grounds of Castelgandolfo. Benedict went immediately to the outer facade to greet the crowds that had gathered to bid him farewell.

Addressing the crowd briefly, the pope thanked them for their presence. Acknowledging that this was a day like no other, the pope asked for their prayers. "I am simply a pilgrim beginning the last leg of his pilgrimage on this earth. But I would still thank you, I would still—with my heart, with my love, with my prayers, with my reflection, and with all my inner strength—like to work for the common good and the good of the Church and of humanity."[2]

At 7:59 p.m. the Swiss Guard withdrew their service of protection for the pope. At 8:00 p.m. the bells at the village Church of St. Thomas tolled the end of Benedict's pontificate. A ripple of applause ran through the crowd as the great oak doors overlooking the square were closed and locked. The pontificate of Benedict XVI that had lasted seven years and ten months was at an end. Most turned away in sadness.

Bergoglio studiously avoided public comments about the forthcoming election but had told Argentina's daily, *La Nación*, that his age precluded him from election. Confident that he would leave Rome shortly after the conclave, he had booked his return ticket, economy class, for March 23.

Shortly before his resignation Pope Benedict published a *motu proprio*, a short letter concerning the next conclave. While Pope John Paul II had decreed in 1996 that fifteen to twenty days could elapse following the vacancy of the Holy See, Benedict allowed the cardinals freedom to change the timescale. On March 1 Cardinal Angelo Sodano sent a message summoning them to Rome.

The cardinals met over a number of days in General Congregations. All who participated in the conclave had been created by John Paul II or Benedict XVI. Only during the *sede vacante* period do the cardinals experience total freedom to speak openly among themselves without the presence of the pope.

The first congregation took place in the Paul VI Audience Hall on the morning of March 4. The cardinals decided to meet twice each day with the exception of Wednesday afternoon, when a prayer service in St. Peter's Basilica would replace the second session.

In his 1996 *Motu Proprio, Universi Domini Gregis,* John Paul II had expressed a firm wish that these meetings remain confidential, thus giving the cardinals an opportunity to discuss issues openly. Each cardinal was allotted five minutes to make a brief intervention on the state of the church.

After the morning meetings on Monday and Tuesday some of the North American cardinals gave press conferences. Cardinals Seán Patrick O'Malley of Boston, Francis George of Chicago, and Daniel Di Nardo of Houston spoke candidly about the challenges in the church and the world. The conferences were attended by a large number of journalists. So popular did the American briefings prove that the English-speaking journalists decamped to the North American College to hear the cardinals speak with unexpected honesty and sincerity. There was also a good deal of good humor.

On Wednesday the press conference was abruptly canceled as some other cardinals objected to the North American initiative. The only other daily press briefings were offered by the spokesman of the Holy See, Jesuit Fr. Federico Lombardi.

The issues confronting the church were enormous. The world's rapidly expanding population required new responses from church leaders to ever-more complex issues. Poverty, human rights, and sexual mores were among the issues that repeatedly surfaced. In many places, notably Europe and Latin America, the number of active Christians was on the wane. In some countries Christians were brutally persecuted. The church faced both challenges and opportunities.

Many of the problems were internal. The inequality that women faced in the church, the leaked documents from Benedict's office, the accusations of money laundering through Vatican institutions, and corruption charges, all needed to be examined openly and resolved. The unwieldy nature of the Roman Curia, in its largely sixteenth-century format, also needed to be addressed. In one of the last interventions at the General Congregation, Cardinal

Bergoglio made a brief four-minute intervention. It was short and to the point.

Following the conclave, Cardinal Jaime Ortega, archbishop of Havana, revealed how impressed the cardinals had been. He recounted how he asked the Argentinian for a copy of his short speech, to which Bergoglio replied that he had spoken off the cuff. The Cuban cardinal pressed Bergoglio to sum up the essence of his intervention. The next day Bergoglio gave Ortega a handwritten copy, not guessing it would become public. Ortega posted the speech on his diocesan website and also circulated the memorandum as an aide-mémoire, evidently hoping to influence his fellow cardinals. In the text, Bergoglio had written:

> When the Church does not come out of herself to evangelize, she becomes self-referential and then gets sick. (cf. The deformed woman of the Gospel). The evils that, over time, happen in ecclesial institutions have their root in self-deference and a kind of theological narcissism. In the Book of the Apocalypse, Jesus says that he stands at the door and knocks. Obviously, the text refers to his knocking from the outside in order to enter but I think about the times in which Jesus knocks from within so that we will let him come out. The self-referential Church keeps Jesus Christ within herself and does not let him out.[3]

These words impressed several cardinals who wondered if it was now time to reconsider the runner-up in the 2005 conclave. Perhaps it was time to move from Europe and launch a search among the American cardinals?

Halfway through the meetings news arrived that Cardinal Keith O'Brien, archbishop of St. Andrews and Edinburgh since 1985, would not attend the forthcoming conclave. In a statement he revealed that "there have been times that my sexual conduct has fallen below the standards expected of me as a priest, archbishop and cardinal." The cardinal's admission was prompted by complaints by some priests who had witnessed his conduct and had brought it to the attention of Archbishop Antonio Mennini, papal nuncio to Britain, and eventually to the media. However, even the shock of these revelations was unable to shift world interest away from filling the vacuum left by Benedict through a medieval system of voting.

Probably less than a dozen of the 115 cardinals entering the conclave were serious candidates. The vast majority were not considered papabile, material to be pope. Age and health were grounds on which most were considered to be excluded.

Journalists settled on a few likely candidates whose cause they promoted. Few believed that Austrian Cardinal Christoph Schönborn of Vienna would be elected because a third pope from middle Europe seemed unlikely. A member of the Dominican Order and a polyglot, he was a competent administrator and respected theologian. Schönborn was also editor of the Catechism of the Catholic Church that Pope John Paul II had promulgated in 1992.

Canadian Cardinal Marc Ouellet, Prefect of the Congregation for Bishops, seemed a likely choice if the new pope was to come from the New World. A former archbishop of Montreal, the sixty-six-year-old Ouellet had worked for a decade in Colombia and was a competent linguist. Two other cardinals from North America were favored by the media, in particular the Italian media. Cardinal Seán Patrick O'Malley of Boston had inherited a diocese in chaos following the resignation of Cardinal Bernard Law in 2002. Law had been implicated in the cover-up of clergy who had sexually abused children and his liability was uncovered in a civil suit. O'Malley's simplicity as a Capuchin friar and his gentle yet jovial manner made him an attractive candidate. Cardinal Timothy Dolan, the gregarious and expansive archbishop of New York, proved popular with journalists who enjoyed his robust good humor.

South America presented a strong character in the person of Pedro Odilo Scherer, archbishop of Sao Paolo. A one-time curial official he was respected for his engagement in the Brazilian church. At sixty-three he promised to have a lengthy pontificate, perhaps too lengthy in some eyes.

If the papacy was to return to the Italians, media sources speculated on Cardinal Angelo Scola of Milan. Ordained for the Communion and Liberation Group founded by Don Luigi Giussani, the scholarly prelate was seen as Italy's best hope. Benedict had also transferred him from Venice to Milan. Both sees had provided several popes in the previous century. It was presumed that he would have been one of Benedict's principal choices to succeed him. Should the cardinals seek a young pontiff and one from Asia, Luis Antonio Tagle, the fifty-five-year-old archbishop of Manila, seemed a good choice. The fact that he had been a cardinal for less than six months would weigh strongly against him. Italians jested that they wanted a Holy Father not an Eternal Father.

Reform of the Curia was a consistent theme, although what that reform would entail was unclear. Sorting out the Institute for Religious Works, erroneously referred to as the Vatican Bank, was also to be a task for the new pope. Declining church attendance in Europe, as well as syncretic practices in South America, were also challenges for the new pope. One observer, Jesuit writer Thomas Reese, summed it up by saying the cardinals wanted Jesus with an MBA!

As the date drew near for the conclave, many cardinals were undecided. Part of their problem was that they hardly knew each other, for most rarely met outside ritual ceremonies in Rome. There was a sense of the "insiders" and the "outsiders." The over eighty-year-olds would wait outside as the electors filed into the Sistine Chapel on the afternoon of March 12. If the conclave was prolonged they faced the prospect of getting to know each other only too well.

CHAPTER SEVEN

The Second Conclave

Light rain was falling in St. Peter's Square on Wednesday, March 13. Already a dense crowd had filled the piazza. It was just half an hour to go until 7:00 p.m. when the ballots were due to be burned in the stove at the rear of the Sistine Chapel. Would there be more black smoke as the second day of the conclave ended? Many people had gathered both the previous evening and that morning to witness black plumes of smoke rising from the chimney. Voices murmured quietly and many were praying.

Inside the Sistine Chapel the new pope had passed the seventy-seven, or two-thirds, votes required to be elected. A warm applause ran through the ranks of the cardinal electors as Bergoglio's name was repeatedly called out by the scrutineer. They had completed their mission, and the church had a new pope.

Cardinal Bergoglio listened as the remaining votes were counted and his name echoed around the chapel. When the final tally had been made, the assistant cardinal dean, Giovanni Battista Re, approached the archbishop of Buenos Aires.

"Do you accept the canonical election?" he asked in Latin. There was a silence as Bergoglio lowered his eyes. After a few moments he looked up.

"I am a great sinner; trusting in God's mercy and patience; in suffering I accept," came the reply.

"And what name do you take?" There was another pause.

"I will be called Francis."

Although most had not heard the exchange, they knew from the spontaneous embrace Cardinal Sodano gave Bergoglio that he had accepted. A more robust applause broke out. The cardinals nearest the new pope passed the name, unusual yet familiar, down the line. This was the first pope to take the name of Francis. Heads nodded, eyebrows rose. For some cardinals it was a signal that he would make his unique mark. Others wondered what they had just done.

Monsignor Guido Marini, papal master of liturgical ceremonies, brought the newly elected pope to the sacristy to the left of the high altar behind Michaelangelo's great fresco of the *Last Judgment*. The papal tailor awaited the new pope with garments in three sizes. The new pope smiled somberly as the tailor genuflected and kissed the pontiff's ring. He assisted the pontiff to change from his scarlet soutane and don the white papal scimar.

The pope declined to wear the red mozzetta, an elbow-length cape worn by the Roman pontiff for more than six hundred years. When offered a gold-jeweled pectoral cross, Pope Francis reached out for the silver metal cross that he had worn since he became bishop in Argentina.

Several white boxes with red leather shoes in a number of sizes were laid out on a table. The tailor asked the pope what size shoe he wore. Pope Francis looked at him. "Why?" he asked. The tailor indicated the traditional red shoes, the shoes of the fisherman. "These are fine with me," Pope Francis said, looking down at his battered black shoes.

Below in St. Peter's Square the crowd waited for the cardinal proto dean, Cardinal Jean Louis Tauran, to announce the news of the election. The ballots were to be burned at 7:00 p.m., and as yet the crowds did not know that the election had taken place.

The iron hand on the clock of the bell tower of St. Peter's moved toward the seventh hour. The rain eased slightly but most umbrellas remained open, strangers sheltering under the colorful canopy. An intense quiet and calm had settled on the crowd. The delay added to the electrical sense of expectation.

Suddenly at 7:06 p.m. smoke began to unfurl from the chimney atop the Sistine Chapel. Large screens had been erected so that the crowds could see.

"*É bianco, il fumo è bianco!*"—"It's white, the smoke is white!"

Excited voices rose in various languages throughout the square. All eyes were fixed on the tiny chimney protruding from the roof of the chapel. There was no doubt. The first, pale wisp was now followed by billowing dense clouds of white smoke. Cheers went up. *Viva il papa*! Nobody yet knew the identity of the new pope. But a pope had been elected—that the church had a leader once more seemed enough for the crowd. The umbrellas raised about the heads of tens of thousands danced as people excitedly exchanged hugs. National flags rose and were waved wildly by scores.

Slowly the great bells of St. Peter's began to toll. Gathering pace, their sound was echoed as all the church bells, silenced since the beginning of the conclave, rang throughout the city. People clapped and hugged, greeting each other in scores of languages. Like waves roaring toward the shore, shouts resounded across the expanse of the square. *Viva il papa*! While millions watched the pageantry on television and internet only those gathered in the square could understand the feeling, the almost electrical jubilation that seemed to crackle in the damp Roman air.

Alerted to the news, thousands of Romans and visitors hastened to St. Peter's. A new bishop had been chosen. As the rain suddenly stopped, all lowered their umbrellas and hoods. Finally the bells ceased, although white smoke continued to pour unabated through the chimney. The crowds moved as one body, surging toward the facade of the basilica. Within moments, the Swiss Guard who were already on alert, marched from the barracks below the Apostolic Palace and up the steps of the basilica. A brass band played a sprightly march. Dispatches of the various Italian military corps, each complete with its brass band, followed immediately. The brightly uniformed soldiers moved with mechanical precision up the steps of the basilica onto the sagrato, the platform underneath the balcony where the new pope would make his first appearance.

Flags from every continent waved through the crowd as people wondered who the new pope would be. Occasionally shouts erupted—long live the pope! *Viva, viva*! The bands continued to play merry marches as the crowds waited patiently. An hour had passed since the unfurling smoke had heralded the election. The rituals had to be observed. First, the pope received the congratulations and obedience of all the cardinals present, standing beside them rather than sitting on the throne prepared in front of the high altar.

Accompanied by cardinal electors, the new pope walked to the sixteenth-century Pauline Chapel to pray before the Blessed Sacrament. On either side of him were Michelangelo's great last frescoes, the martyrdom of St. Peter and

St. Paul. The cardinals sang a *Te Deum* in gratitude for the new pope while the first Latin American pope knelt in front of the tabernacle.

It was now time for Francis to present himself to the people of Rome, even though the square was thronged with foreigners. The windows in the upper corridor of the facade lit up. Soon the announcement would be made. Across the world, television and radio networks broadcast the unfolding events.

As he walked along the corridor leading to the balcony, Pope Francis paused and asked to telephone his predecessor at Castelgandolfo. After a few moments hesitation, a phone was located and the call put through.

Pope Benedict, with his household, was watching the events on television. They paid little attention to the phone ringing in the background, not wishing to miss the moment when the new pope appeared on the screen. The phone continued to ring. It took several minutes before it occurred to an aide, seated beside the retired pope, that it might be an important phone call. "It's the new pope," whispered Benedict's aide as he handed the phone to the pope emeritus. Once more, history would be made as the new pope and the pope emeritus greeted each other for the first time and offered good wishes and assurances of prayers for one another.

The red velvet curtains parted on the central balcony. Cardinal Jean Louis Tauran emerged onto the loggia. Dazzled by the bright lights, he proclaimed the ancient words: "*Annuntio vobis gaudium magnum. Habemus Papam.*"— "I announce to you great news. We have a pope."

The crowd roared once more with delight, while waving flags wildly in the hope that the new pope might be from their homeland.

"*Eminentissimum ac Reverendissimum Dominum, Dominum Georgium Marium Sanctae Romanae Ecclesiae Cardinalem Bergoglio qui sibi nomen imposuit Francisum.*"—"The most eminent and most reverend Lord Cardinal of the Holy Roman Church, the Lord Jorge Mario Bergoglio, who has taken the name Francis."

The crowd was silent for a moment before roars erupted again of the now familiar *Viva il papa*. With a name like Bergoglio was he Italian? But soon word spread. The pope is from Argentina, the first Latino pope! Shouts swooped up and down in the crowds. The South Americans began singing national songs. Those who had room jumped up and down with joy. For the Italians, it was enough that he had an Italian name. And the choice of their national patron saint as his papal name was even better. Here and there the plainchant tones of the "Salve Regina" floated from sallow-skinned seminarians. The chant of Francesco's name rebounded throughout the square from thousands of voices.

Within moments a red velvet and silk-embroidered drape was hung from the balcony and shortly the red velvet curtains on the balcony parted once more. A large, medieval crucifix was carried out ahead of the new pope. The crowd would soon see the new Roman pontiff. The cheers rose once again, echoing around the square. "Francesco, Francesco, Francesco!"

When he appeared on the balcony the pope seemed overwhelmed by the sight of more than 100,000 cheering faces. He raised his right hand in an uncertain salute and stood uneasily to attention as the brass bands below played the Italian and Vatican anthems. The cardinals gathered on the adjacent balconies to see the reaction of the crowd to their new pope.

"*Buona sera*!" The prosaic greeting, warm and understated, drew delighted laughs from the crowd. For the Italians, he was one of them. "You know," he continued after a moment, "it's the duty of the cardinals to find a new pope. Well, it seems that they went almost to the end of the world to find him, but, here we are!"

Thanking everyone for the warm welcome Francis directed his first thoughts to his predecessor. Inviting the people to pray simple prayers, the Our Father, Hail Mary, and Glory Be, he drew the crowd into one voice. Francis offered his blessing, but first asked the people to pray to God for him in silence:

"Now I will bless you. But I'd like to ask you a favor, for your prayer to bless me as your bishop. Let's pray silently, your prayer for me." He bowed his head. There was intense silence as the thousands in the square and people of goodwill throughout the world prayed for the diminutive figure.

"I am going to bless you all and the entire world—all the men and women of goodwill." Placing a red stole on his shoulders the new bishop of Rome traced the triple sign of the cross as he gave his blessing in Latin. The crowd continued to cheer and sing. "I'm going to leave you now. Good night, and I wish you peace."

By now sharp-eyed observers had noted that Francis had eschewed the traditional pontifical mantel and wore a simple metal cross. Changes were in the air.

Turning to leave, the pope took the microphone again. Promising to make a visit the next day to a Marian church, he waved to the crowds. "We'll see each other soon. Good night and sleep well!"

The address had lasted less than five minutes but it was a foretaste of the power and control that Francis was to wield during his pontificate. The media pundits were largely mistaken about the candidates, and television and radio channels, with ill-prepared reporters, floundered trying to find information about the unforeseen pope. So certain were some Italians that Cardinal Scola would be elected that an excited press officer for the Italian Episcopal Conference hit the "send" button on the fax machine, distributing pre-prepared congratulations on the election of the archbishop of Milan to the papacy.

Beside Pope Francis stood Cardinal Agostino Vallini, the vicar of Rome, and Brazilian Cardinal Cláudio Hummes, who had sat beside him during the conclave. "You are the Vicar of Rome," the pope had told Vallini in the Sistine Chapel. "You must come with me and help me."

It was now time for dinner. Although guided to the black Mercedes in the lower courtyard, Francis ambled instead toward the minibus in which the cardinals returned to their residence. Seated in the middle of the cardinals, he chatted with them on the six-minute journey.

After supper the new pope retired to his quarters. But sleep evidently eluded him; when the other cardinals had gone to their rooms Francis emerged, dressed in black trousers and a black overcoat. He asked if there was a car available because he wanted to go for a drive. An astonished driver fetched a car and shortly afterward the unmarked car exited the gate of the holy office to the side of St. Peter's Basilica. Little could the crowds that had wildly saluted him a couple of hours earlier know that the new pope, from the inside of a small Italian-made car, was watching them with an amused expression on his face.

The next morning at 5:45 Francis emerged from his room. Again dressed in his black trousers, black shoes, and black pullover, he asked the single Swiss Guard on duty what time breakfast was served. The guard replied from 6:30 onward but offered to fetch a coffee. The pope smiled and said he would wait till then and made his way down the corridor to the chapel.

A couple of hours later, having breakfasted with six cardinals who were also early risers, he was off to the Basilica of St. Mary Major. Here he prayed before an icon of the Virgin Mary, *Salus Populi Romani*—the Well-Being of the Romans. The ancient image has been venerated for centuries in Rome's fifth-century basilica dedicated to the honor of Mary. For every journey or important event of his pontificate Francis will return to this shrine.

When the security officers tried to close the basilica to the public Francis stopped them. "Leave them alone. I am a pilgrim too." As he left the church he met the confessors, urging them always to be merciful to penitents who come to avail themselves of the sacrament of penance and reconciliation. Boarding his car outside the basilica he looked up to the windows of the school overlooking the church. As the children screamed loudly, the pope made hand signals that he would come one day to visit them.

Leaving St. Mary's he then went to collect his luggage at the clerical hostel on the Via del Clero beside Piazza Navona. Arriving at the Casa del Clero, the pope asked at the porter's desk for a bulb for the bedside lamp that had blown some days earlier. The surprised official gave the pope the bulb. A short while later the pope descended with his luggage, paid the bill, saluted everyone, and returned to the Vatican. The bulb had been changed.

CHAPTER EIGHT

A Pontificate Begins

Two days following his election, Pope Francis invited the media to a special audience in Paul VI Hall. Most were already packing up cameras and closing media centers that had focused world attention on the tiny city state. Previous popes had thanked the journalists and their entourages for their coverage of the election. When Francis came out the front door of the Domus Sanctae Marthae where he had been staying, he was surprised to see a large car and escort. Paul VI Hall was only about 550 yards away. With his by now unmistakable arched eyebrows the pope laughed and waved the car away and took off with his lumbering gait toward the hall.

The Vatican officials looked at each other in barely concealed exasperation. Shrugging helplessly, they set off after the leader of the world's 1.2 billion Catholics. Used to controlling every movement of the ailing John Paul II and the docile Benedict, the officials realized that the stubborn Argentinian promised to be a handful.

In a break in his prepared text, the pope explained to the five thousand media personnel that had covered the conclave his reason for selecting the name "Francis." "Let me tell you a story," the pope began. Francis recounted how he sat listening to the votes echo around the Sistine Chapel as they passed the two-thirds majority. During those moments, Cardinal Cláudio Hummes, former archbishop of Sao Paolo, leaned over and whispered, "Jorge, don't forget the poor!" Francis then recalled the patron saint of Italy, the thirteenth-century figure who rejected the riches of his father's home in order to live with the sick and needy: "The man of the poor. The man of peace. The man who loved and cared for creation—and in this moment we don't have such a great relationship with creation. The man who gives us this spirit of peace, the poor man. Ah—how I would like a Church which is poor and for the poor!"

Francis (born ca. 1181) was the son of a prosperous fabric merchant in the Umbrian town of Assisi. He was wounded as a soldier in a battle between the forces of Assisi and Perugia. During his recuperation the young man experienced a change of character. No longer a carefree youth, he now took an active interest in the poor and sick. Gathering a group of like-minded men around him, Francis encouraged them to look after the poor of the district. They wore simple clothing, lived simply, and went about preaching in simple language in the marketplaces and streets of the towns.

Francis attracted scores of followers who enrolled in his band, which was soon supported by Pope Innocent III. Francis's cheerful demeanor earned him the soubriquet *God's troubadour*. Yet when he died he was found to have developed lesions on his side, hands, and feet, similar to the markings of the crucified Jesus.

Francis died in 1226, and just two years later was canonized by Pope Gregory IX. With papal approval, the order of friars continued to flourish after his death. Although there were subsequent divisions, the Franciscans remain one of the most respected orders in the church and Francis was proclaimed the patron saint of Italy. The new pope did not mention that his paternal great-grandfather was named Francesco, and that the name was favored in the Bergoglio family.

Pope Francis revealed that some cardinals subsequently jested that he should have taken other names. "How about Adrian IV, the great reformer?" This was a reference to the need to reform much of the Vatican bureaucracy. Another name they suggested was Clement XV, in remembrance of Clement XIV, who had suppressed the Jesuits in 1773. Lest anyone be under the illusion that he might be serious, he added with a broad grin that these were good-natured jokes.

As he took his leave of the media personnel, he offered his blessing. Speaking in Spanish, he added: "I told you I was cordially imparting my blessing. Since many of you are not members of the Catholic Church and others are not believers, I cordially give this blessing silently, to each of you, respecting the conscience of each, but in the knowledge that each of you is a child of God. May God bless you!"

On the first Sunday of his pontificate Francis celebrated Mass in the parish church of St. Anna. Arriving at the church, which lies at the entrance to the Vatican, the pope went to greet the people who could not gain access to the crowded church. Speaking off the cuff during Mass, Francis spoke of the mercy of God: "While we are prone to judge and not help, God's mercy can help us get over our weakness and help those in deeper need."

At the end of the Mass he introduced a number of priests who had come to concelebrate, laughing while explaining that these were not members of the Vatican parish but rather had sneaked their way in. He took particular pleasure in introducing a priest from Argentina who worked with young people and tried to help them overcome problems with drugs.

> I want to introduce to you a priest who comes from far away, a priest who works with children and with drug addicts on the street. He opened a school for them; he has done many things to make Jesus known, and all those boys and girls off the street, they today work with the studies they have done; they have the ability to work, they believe and they love Jesus. I ask you, Gonzalo, come greet the people: pray for him. He works in Uruguay; he is the founder of *Jubilar Juan Pablo II*. This is his work. I do not know how he came here, but I will find out! Thanks. Pray for him.[1]

No congregation had ever heard a pope speak like this and laughed as the pope gestured and waved to the priests. Following the Mass, while still in his vestments, the pope went to the gates of the Vatican. To the horror of his security personnel he lunged into the crowds, shaking hands and hugging some people whom he recognized. To the senior Vatican authorities the greatest problem was the fact that he had crossed into Italian territory without any regard for protocol. Left unchecked, this would create a diplomatic and security nightmare.

Father Adolfo Nicolás, general of the Society of Jesus, wrote to Francis, offering his congratulations and the good wishes of the confreres. Pope Francis phoned the general and asked him to visit the next day at the Domus Sanctae Marthae. When the two met, the pope insisted that the general desist from addressing him as Holy Father or Your Holiness.

"I am a Jesuit!" bantered Francis.

The general knew that some had greeted Bergoglio's election with emotions ranging from shock to dismay but assured the pope that he could count on the loyalty of the largest male religious congregation, working in 112 countries on six continents.

The new pope was not an outsider to the Vatican. For many years he had been a member of several Vatican congregations, including the commission for Latin America, although he rarely attended the annual plenary meetings in Rome. When asked why he left Rome after only a short visit, on each occasion he jested, "I must get back to my wife, the diocese!" A man lacking in ambition, he had no interest in joining cliques to push one or another agenda.

In the early days of his pontificate the pope often used the phone to contact friends. On the night of his election he was unable to get through to his sister in Argentina as her phone was continuously engaged with other well-wishers. A few days later, the pope's former dentist received a call from the Vatican. The pope thanked him for his years of care, adding that he hoped they would meet again soon.

For some twenty years Daniel Del Regno had delivered a newspaper to the bishop of Buenos Aires. When Pope Francis stepped out on the balcony of St. Peter's on the night of his election, Del Regno realized that he had lost a customer. A phone call confirmed his fears. Although the voice claimed to be that of the new pope, the vendor was sure it was a friend playing a practical joke. "No, truly, this is Jorge Bergoglio!" Speaking to the Argentine daily *La Nación*, Del Regno recounted the moment when he realized that it was indeed the pope, who proceeded to thank him for his years of faithful delivery and sent his good wishes to the Del Regno family.

In his first written message, Pope Francis addressed the Jewish community of Rome. The community is one of the oldest outside the Holy Land. To mark the approaching feast of Passover the pope sent a letter to Rabbi Riccardo Di Segni, thanking the rabbi of the Roman synagogue for his good wishes and expressing the hope of working together.

In Jorge Bergoglio's native country people needed to be up early to watch the Mass to mark the beginning of the Petrine ministry. Thousands crowded into the park in front of the cathedral of Buenos Aires. The morning dew still clung to the grass and trees. Large screens were erected in the square so the crowds could see the broadcast from Rome. Several wrapped themselves in the blue and white national flag.

Shortly before the Mass began, a familiar voice came over the loudspeakers. A cheer went up as the crowd recognized the familiar voice. The pope was on the telephone.

"I want to ask you to walk together, and take care of one another," said the voice. "Do not cause harm. Protect life. Protect the family; protect nature; protect the young; protect the elderly. Let there not be hatred or fighting. Put aside envy. Don't take the hide off anybody." The crowds laughed at the familiar folksy expression. "Talk with one another so that this desire to protect each other might grow in your hearts. And draw near to God. God is good. He always forgives and understands. And don't forget that this bishop who is far away loves you very much. Pray for me."

Spring had been unseasonably cold and wet in Italy. Yet on March 19, the day of the Mass to mark the beginning of the Petrine ministry, the sun shone brilliantly, and St. Peter's Square was filled to capacity. The pope wore a simple unadorned chasuble rather than the traditional elaborate vestments.

Although the pope had asked the papal nuncio in Argentina to dissuade people and clergy from traveling to Rome from Argentina, there was a small delegation from the archdiocese. Among them was Sergio Sánchez, a young man whose journey had been paid for by a benefactor. A *cartonero,* a poor man who makes money from collecting scrap paper, Sergio belonged to the Excluded Workers Alliance. He had often met Archbishop Bergoglio on his visits to the slums of the city.

When Francis emerged from the basilica to the steps where Mass would be celebrated, the pope was visibly surprised and gave a warm welcome to his fellow Argentinian. During the Mass, Cardinal Angelo Sodano placed the pallium of office on his shoulders and the ring of the fisherman on his finger. With typical frugality, Francis had refused to commission a ring but used a silver ring made for Pope Paul VI thirty-five years earlier by the artist Enrico Manfrini.

To honor the presence of Bartholomew I, the patriarch of Constantinople, the gospel was proclaimed in Greek. Meeting with ecumenical delegates the following morning, the pope thanked them all for coming. Bartholomew I met with the pope privately for twenty minutes when the two agreed to travel to Jerusalem together in 2014 to mark the fiftieth anniversary of the meeting of Pope Paul VI and Patriarch Athenagoras.

That afternoon the pope hosted friends and members of the Argentinian community in Rome. His two fellow natives of Buenos Aires, Cardinal Leonardo Sandri and Archbishop Marcelo Sánchez Sorondo, joined a hundred well-wishers, and the pope was presented with a jersey of his beloved San Lorenzo Football Club. The pope quipped that he had not missed a single championship club match since 1946. "There are not many fans who can say that," Francis said with a laugh. "Don't make me miss them now!

The next morning, the pope celebrated Mass at 7:00 at the Domus Sanctae Marthae. Almost all the cardinals had left and the pope remarked that the house seemed quite empty. The previous day he had requested Archbishop Georg Gaenswein to invite some people to the morning Mass. Thus the cooks and cleaners of the domus were invited to the Mass in the main chapel that the cardinals had vacated.

This was the beginning of a new way of celebrating Mass. While Pope John Paul II regularly invited people to Mass in the Apostolic Palace, Pope Benedict XVI rarely invited guests. For Francis, the chapel was open to everybody. The following day, the street cleaners, garbage collectors, and gardeners of the Vatican were invited. Later that morning, Luciano Cecchetti, one of the gardeners, expressed his disbelief at the invitation: "Usually we're the invisible and forgotten ones."

Each morning the pope continued the practice of inviting various workers in the Vatican, stopping to greet each one personally after Mass. Throughout the pontificate the brief homilies became a way in which the pope communicated his thoughts—the text was scrutinized by people to understand them.

It was a sight never before seen in 2,000 years of Christian history. While a handful of popes have abdicated, there is no record of any meeting between successor and predecessor. On Saturday morning, March 23, Francis left the Vatican by helicopter bound for Castelgandolfo to visit the pope emeritus in the country residence.

Arriving at the landing pad at Castelgandolfo, Pope Francis was surprised that Benedict had come to greet him personally. Emerging from the helicopter, Francis saw the elderly pontiff emeritus standing in the cold morning air. The retired pontiff wore a simple white soutane, with a white quilted Parka jacket to ward off the chill of the March day.

"Good morning! Thank you for your visit," said Benedict as he welcomed his guest. He appeared considerably frailer than when he had made his last public appearance three weeks earlier. Francis smiled back. There was no protocol to govern the historic meeting. But this was a meeting between two old friends.

Turning to the car the pair made the brief journey to the main villa. Entering on the ground floor they were accompanied to the chapel on the floor above. Benedict stood back to allow Francis to enter the chapel. The latter was evidently slightly nervous. Benedict followed him, walking slowly with a cane and indicated that he would kneel behind the pope. Francis turned toward the back of the chapel. "No, no," Benedict gestured toward the pontiff to kneel in the front. Francis took his hand. "Please, let us pray together. We are brothers." Touched by the new pope's kindness, Benedict knelt beside Francis. No protocol could have foreseen the simplicity of the two pontiffs joined together in prayer before the tabernacle.

As a guest of the former pope, Francis brought a gift. With disarming candor he admitted that the gift, an icon of the Madonna, had been chosen for him by his aides. "It is the Madonna of Humility," he explained. "I did not know it before. If you don't mind my saying, it reminds me of the many signs of humility you gave us in your pontificate." Benedict murmured his thanks, "Grazie, grazie!"

The two men then withdrew for a private dialogue for three-quarters of an hour before lunching with the secretaries. Benedict personally renewed his obedience to the new pope. As he left Castelgandolfo, the new pope took a large carton containing the files of the three cardinals who had investigated the crimes committed by the former papal butler. During their colloquy, Benedict had given Francis a concise synopsis of the contents of the report. This brought the dramatic period of forty days of church events to a close.

In the Christian calendar Palm Sunday marks the beginning of the annual commemoration of the last week of Jesus' life. Recalling the entrance into Jerusalem, the people of Rome gather around the bishop in St. Peter's Square to re-enact the jubilant day two thousand years earlier when Jesus received an ecstatic welcome to Jerusalem.

For Francis, this was another opportunity to meet with the immense crowds that packed St. Peter's Square. In his homily during Mass the pope announced that he would travel to Brazil in July to attend the World Youth Day. For the first time in twenty-five years the World Youth Day would be held in South America. The Latin American pope was going home. Within days, the Vatican office organizing the World Youth Day in Rio de Janeiro was overwhelmed with calls and e-mails concerning the July event. Bookings surged upward, indicating that as many as two million young people would attend the ceremonies, which would be spread over the week of July 22–28.

After the Mass, Pope Francis traveled through the crowds on the popemobile, asking the driver to stop on several occasions. He disembarked when he recognized some young people from Buenos Aires who vivaciously hugged and kissed him. When an elderly woman reached out to touch him, he held her hand and kissed it.

Holy Week is the most sacred liturgical period in the church year when Christians commemorate the death and resurrection of Jesus. The Jewish Passover, or Pesach, fell during the same days, and Francis sent his greetings to the Jewish community in Rome. It was the second time he had greeted Rabbi Di Segno in a week.

On the Monday of Holy Week most of the forty priests and bishops who normally live in the Domus Sanctae Marthae returned to their rooms that they had vacated to make way for the cardinals during the conclave. The priests mostly serve in the secretariat of state or other offices. Although they knew the pope was still in residence they were surprised to be invited to Mass the following morning in the residence chapel. Pope Francis said how much he enjoyed being in the Domus and sharing the fraternity with those who lived there. He indicated that he would not move into the private apartments in the Apostolic Palace, where previous popes had lived. When he had visited the private apartments following his election, he had exclaimed that three hundred people could live in the space. In an interview some months later he joked that he enjoyed the company of other people and that this was simply to keep him sane.

When Mass was over the pope sat in the last bench at the back of the chapel. As the priests left he stood and greeted each personally, thanking him for his service.

Upon taking his leave, he left a large Easter egg, which he had received, as a gift to the clergy. The priests were bemused by the new tenant. In the coming weeks Francis would become a familiar figure sitting at a round table with a glass of orange juice in his hand, laughing and gesticulating with residents and visitors alike. He would take his place in the line for food at breakfast, lunch, and dinner, sitting wherever he found a space. The security detail observed the scene and tried to adapt as best they could.

St. Peter's Square was filled by thousands who attended the first Wednesday general audience. Francis pointedly spoke only in Italian, understood by some to underline his commitment to the Italian citizens of Rome. Such were the crowds that Francis toured the entire perimeter to salute the people. Before leaving, the pope saluted the disabled who were in attendance and even signed his name on the plaster cast of a young girl who had broken her leg.

On Holy Thursday, the pope presided over the Chrism Mass in St. Peter's Basilica. Bishops and priests attended the annual Mass at which the holy oils used in the administration of the sacraments were blessed. In his homily the new pontiff gave the first hint of his expectations of priests. His message was demanding and critical of priests who do not fulfill their ministry. "We need to go out to the outskirts where there is suffering, bloodshed, blindness that longs for sight, and prisoners enthralled to many evil masters." By doing this, priests could be sure of the support of the people.

Francis continued: "Those who do not go out of themselves, instead of being mediators, gradually become intermediaries, managers. We know the difference: the intermediary, the manager, 'has already received his reward,' and since he doesn't put his own skin and his own heart on the line, he never hears a warm, heartfelt word of thanks. This is precisely the reason for the dissatisfaction of some, who end up sad—sad priests— in some sense becoming collectors of antiques or novelties, instead of being shepherds living with the smell of the sheep."[2]

For those who knew Bergoglio, these sharp words were familiar echoes of his high standards as a Jesuit superior and diocesan bishop in Argentina.

Meeting Archbishop Giovanni Becciu, deputy secretary of state, after Mass, the pontiff asked him what he was doing for lunch. "I am having some priests over to my apartment for a meal," the archbishop said. It was a tradition he had kept up since he was apostolic nuncio in Angola and Cuba. "May I come too?" came the unexpected request. The guests were mostly from the parishes of Rome. One was Don Angelo Donatis, rector of the Parish of San Marco in Campidoglio, a well-known spiritual adviser to priests in the city. Monsignor Enrico Feroci, director of Caritas, the social outreach program for the poor of the Diocese of Rome, was another guest. The other clergy worked with the poor and marginalized. The atmosphere at the table was relaxed. Pope Francis recalled several anecdotes of his life in Argentina. Before he left the priests, he advised them to pay particular attention to the sacrament of penance and reconciliation. The idea occurred to him to write a letter to the homeless. When asked how it could be delivered, he said the priests could give it personally. "Put the light on the confessional. You will see the people form a line when they see it," he advised.

On Thursday afternoon Francis broke a centuries-old tradition. Rather than celebrate the Mass of the Lord's Supper, the opening of the Easter Triduum, in the baroque splendor of St. Peter's Basilica, the pope visited the youth detention center in a Roman suburb. During his years as bishop in Buenos Aires, Jorge Bergoglio celebrated Mass with the poor and the sick. As he left the Vatican with Cardinal Agostino Vallini, vicar of the Diocese of Rome, the roads were lined with well-wishers. The pope kept repeating the words "incredible, incredible" as he looked out the window at the enthusiastic crowds.

The pope had asked that only the fifty residents detained at the center attend. Of that number, only eight were Italian and only some were Catholic. A Caritas volunteer overheard one of the young detainees react to the unexpected news of the visit by saying, "At last I will get to meet somebody who claims he is my father!" For the first time in a papal liturgy, the pope washed the feet of Muslims and of a young girl. Before he left, the pope gave presents of Easter eggs and colomba, the traditional Easter cake.

Soon the pope settled into a routine. Those who lived in the Domus Sanctae Marthae were somewhat bewildered at their illustrious guest. Despite the efforts of the security guards, the residents regularly crossed paths with the pope. It was not unusual when the elevator doors opened to reveal the pope alone. Some of the residents were also irritated at the increased security that now surrounded the house and occasionally made access difficult.

Francis took the change in stride. Seeing a Swiss Guard standing outside his room one evening, the pope suggested that he be seated. The young guard replied that he was obliged to guard the pope during the night and had to remain standing. The pope went into his room and brought out a chair. "I am going to bed," he said. "I can give you an order to sit down." The young guard was perplexed but finally obeyed. Some moments later the pope returned with a snack. "Standing there, you must be hungry," he said, before wishing the guard a good night.

Each morning Francis celebrated Mass at 7:00 and continued to invite people who worked in Vatican City State. He often preached off the cuff on the scriptural readings. Observers noted both his style and the content. There was enough interest in these informal homilies that Vatican television began to broadcast them on the Vatican news website. The brief meditations were suitable for sound bites.

At the general audiences the pope bantered with the crowds, especially in his exchanges among young people. He regularly broke away from his prepared text to recount an anecdote or to offer a brief reflection. Often these were provocative. Citing the gospel where Jesus urges a welcome for the stranger, the pope paused. "That is true. Welcome the stranger. How many foreigners are there in this Diocese of Rome? Yes, and what do we do for them?" He shrugged his shoulders.

The enormous numbers that attended the public ceremonies and audiences showed no sign of abating. Although he had learned German, French, and English he felt uncomfortable speaking them. He often excused his accent, explaining that English gave him most difficulty. But his homely Italian charmed everybody.

Vatican officials were getting used to Pope Francis's eccentricities. Noticing that all the lights were on in the apostolic library one sunny morning, he asked an assistant to turn them off. "That will keep the bills down," he commented wryly.

At the Domus Sanctae Marthae the pope also insisted on turning lights off in the corridors when there was nobody around. One exasperated curial official complained to a colleague, "The Latin American bishops are always difficult to deal with but a Latino pope is just impossible!"

In early April the pope formally took possession of the cathedral of Rome, St. John Lateran. Built in the early fourth century by Emperor Constantine, the Lateran Basilica and palace had served as the bishop's cathedral and residence for a millennium. Entering the basilica, the pope was almost mobbed by the crowds. With a broad smile, Pope Francis lunged into the outstretched arms.

During the Mass the pope carried the aluminum pastoral staff made in 1965 for Pope Paul VI by the Neapolitan sculptor Lillo Scorzelli. Benedict XVI ceased using the austere cross when he received a gift of a more traditional ferula cross in 2009 from the Circle of St. Peter, a charitable confraternity founded in 1869. The return to the simple crucifix that had also been used by John Paul I and John Paul II seemed to be a further rupture from the liturgy as had been celebrated by Pope Benedict.

Pope Francis reiterated the message the following Sunday when he ordained ten men in St. Peter's Basilica, exhorting the new priests to be "pastors, not functionaries, mediators, not intermediaries."

The pope began a series of Sunday morning visits to the 335 parishes of Rome, following his meeting with ecclesial groups on Pentecost in May. The first parish, Santi Elisabetta e Zaccaria, was on the periphery of Rome. As was his custom in Buenos Aires, the pontiff gave the children of the parish their First Communion during Mass. The morning visit was carried out with the utmost simplicity. Because of the crowds Mass had to be celebrated in the open air. The pope bantered with the children before he took his leave to recite the midday Angelus with the crowds waiting in St. Peter's Square.

Although no longer administering an Argentinian diocese of 2.5 million, Francis continued in the style and conviction developed over a lifetime. Just two days prior to his election, he had quietly observed fifty-five years since he began his training with the Jesuits, and on April 22 he marked the fortieth anniversary of his final profession. He also had to deal with a bout of painful sciatica from which he had suffered for years. "I would not wish this on my enemies," Francis said to residents of the Domus Sanctae Marthae who sympathized with him when they saw him hobbling along the corridor.

Cardinal Bergoglio had been contemplating his imminent retirement when he heard of Benedict XVI's resignation. Now he had responsibility for the world's 1.2 billion Catholics as well as other Christians and members of the world's faiths. The distribution of Catholics globally was uneven. The greatest concentrations were in Brazil, Mexico, Philippines, North America, and Italy. The previous century had seen unprecedented growth in the Catholic population of the world, from an estimated 291 million in 1910 to 1.1

billion in 2010. The world's population had grown enormously over the century too, and in 2010 Catholics comprised 50 percent of all Christians and just over 16 percent of humanity. The distribution of Catholics had shifted dramatically during the century. In 1910 two-thirds of the world's Catholics lived in Europe, but by 2010 only a quarter of the Catholic population lived in Europe; the largest distribution of 39 percent was found in Latin America and the Caribbean. This change required the close attention of the new pope.

Within two weeks of his election Francis personally appointed his former auxiliary bishop, Mario Aurelio Poli, as his successor. In February 2014 he included the archbishop in his list of nineteen new cardinals.

While he could not compete with the high theology of his predecessor, the "Professor Pope," Francis's simple and brief homilies and speeches gained attention. Although Francis consistently referred to himself as bishop of Rome, the role was not simply confined to the diocese. Since the first century the administration at Rome intervened in the affairs of other dioceses. That waxed and waned during subsequent centuries. In the twentieth century, papal power reached its highest point under John Paul II, whose global journeys covered some 698,310 miles—twenty-eight times around the earth or three times the distance between the earth and moon. Karol Wojtyla's energy was legendary. He was fifty-eight when he was elected to the papacy; Jorge Bergoglio was already seventy-six.

A month after his election Francis turned his attention to pressing matters of administration. If his pontificate was to be more than gestures he needed to provide firm governance and needed to address the "Vatileaks" document that had partially caused Benedict's abdication.

It was clear the Curia, which assisted the pope in his pastoral care of the church, needed an overhaul. The last time a reform of the Curia had been undertaken was by Pope Paul VI in his Apostolic Constitution, *Regimini Ecclesiae Universae*, published in 1967. Establishing a committee of eight cardinals from five continents to assist him, Pope Francis's advisory board included Francisco Javier Errázuriz Ossa of Santiago, Oswald Gracias of Bombay, Reinhard Marx of Munich, Laurent Monsengwo Pasinya of Kinshasa, Seán Patrick O'Malley of Boston, George Pell of Sydney, and Giuseppe Bertello, governor of Vatican City State. Óscar Andrés Rodríguez Maradiaga of Tegucigalpa, Honduras, was appointed to coordinate the group.

This form of consultation had not been seen in over a millennium, when the five patriarchs of Rome, Constantinople, Alexandria, Jerusalem, and Antioch were in regular correspondence. While the pope intended that the group meet four times a year, he also consulted regularly with them by telephone and mail. Former colleagues recalled that although Bergoglio consulted widely he always made decisions alone. His Jesuit training of discernment came to the fore, as he considered from all angles the various situations presented to him.

Many hoped that with a Latin pope outmoded forms of ecclesiastical offices and exaggerated forms of address and offices would be abolished. The contribution of women in the church needed to be fostered and acknowledged with more than mere lip service, and Francis seemed to promise much in this regard. The pope indicated that he would be open to hear from national bishops' conferences about the issue of obligatory celibacy for diocesan clergy if they wished to discuss their regional situation.

Pope Francis's swift and firm resolution of banking scandals he had inherited as archbishop of Buenos Aires prepared him well for restructuring of the Vatican's financial system, which had long been exploited by dishonest clients. Such changes would help end the damaging careerism that saw clergy spend their whole working lives in offices that were only intended for a five-year term. Jesuits make a promise to avoid high ecclesiastical office. For Jorge Bergoglio, such careerism in any part of the church was not acceptable.

The global face of Catholicism continued to develop and change. There was the problem of persecuted Catholics and Christians in various countries, the underground church in China, the scandal of clerical pedophilia, waning ecumenism, and loss of faith in former Christian countries. In addition, Francis's attention would be needed for the thousands of Latino Catholics in both South and North America who abandoned their native faith in favor of the ever-expanding evangelical sects. When meeting with Latin American bishops for their annual visit at the end of April 2013, he urged them not to produce more documents but a plan to engage with people.

Francis's election corresponded with the Year of Faith that Benedict XVI had inaugurated in 2012 to mark the fiftieth anniversary of the Second Vatican Council. For Francis, these months provided an opportunity to encourage the people to remain firm and deepen their Catholic faith. On June 29, 2013, to mark the closure of the celebration, Pope Francis published his first encyclical, *Lumen Fidei,* Light of Faith. The body of the text had been prepared by Pope Benedict XVI, and Francis added some smaller additions. It was designed to complete a trilogy on hope and charity.

It was inevitable that Francis's election would not be met with universal approval; although having enjoyed such a promising start Francis was bound to disappoint some people. In his own country calls from the mothers and grandmothers of the victims of the Dirty Wars called on his intervention.

But even a pope could not unravel the horrific threads of murder and torture carried out by the military juntas.

The pope pushed forward the beatification of Archbishop Oscar Romero of El Salvador, the outspoken and tenacious proponent of human rights, who had been assassinated while celebrating Mass on March 24, 1980. The pope's intervention unblocked the cause that had stalled it for several years, one more signal of the direction the pontificate was taking.

By now three of Francis's siblings had died, leaving him with one remaining sister, María Elena. In May 2010 his brother Alberto Horacio had died. His late sister Marta, who had died in 2007, had two sons and a daughter with her husband Enrico Narvaja: Pablo, a teacher; José Luis, who, like his uncle, had become a Jesuit; and María Inés. María Elena had two sons, Juan and Jorge. She invited her brother to become Jorge's godfather. But he was far from his "spouse" Buenos Aires and physically separated from his people. He could no longer experience the smells, the noises, and the hustle and bustle of his native land. Many who knew Bergoglio well noted that he did not seem to have close friends. He was on friendly terms with many but he seemed extremely self-sufficient. Despite his fondness for the telephone, it would never be a substitute for those face-to-face encounters on which he had thrived. Now an elderly man, an enormous task awaited him—engaging the hopes and expectations of millions.

The eloquent proponent of liberation theology, Leonardo Boff, pithily summed up the extraordinary events that led the first Latino pope to the throne of Peter: "What matters isn't Bergoglio and his past, but Francis and his future.[3]

Slowly the Vatican authorities became used to the unusual habits of the Argentinian pope. On June 7 parents, students, teachers, and past pupils of Jesuit schools in Italy and

Albania were received in Paul VI Audience Hall. As Francis took his seat, Archbishop Gaenswein handed him his script. Looking around him at the vivacious audience he began, "I prepared this address for you . . . but it is five pages long! And it's pretty boring! Let's do something else: Let's see if it will be possible for a few of you to ask a question and we can have a little dialogue. Do we like this idea or not? Yes? Good. Let's follow this route."

The organizers froze with fear. They had not anticipated this.

The former schoolteacher found himself perfectly at ease as he spoke to the young people. "Above all there is something I want to say to you: Never let yourselves be robbed of hope. Let nobody ever rob this from you. Keep your hope, keep your hearts open to the future!"

The grandson of migrants, Jorge Bergoglio had a special interest in displaced people. When he learned of the plight of Africans who risked a shipwreck, crossing into Europe, the pope paid a short visit to the island Lampedusa. It was his first trip outside Rome since his election. The Italian island lies about eighty miles off the coast of Tunisia, and thousands of immigrants wash up on its shores each year. The rickety wooden boats, exposed to the elements, were run by pirates who insisted that the refugees pay exorbitant prices. On the morning of July 8 the pope met with survivors, mostly Muslim, and celebrated Mass on an upturned boat. The visit served to focus global indifference on the humanitarian problem, for most leaving Africa risked a precarious existence in Europe, which was in economic crisis.

Francis appointed a Polish priest as papal almoner to dispense charity to the needy. Although the office had existed for centuries, in recent years it had limited itself to paying bills for needy people in Rome. Francis told Monsignor

Konrad Krajewski, whom he ordained a bishop, that he wanted him to go out on the streets and meet poor people. "I can't go out like you can," the pope told Krajewski, "so I am entrusting you to be my eyes and hands." Funds were provided for Krajewsk to distribute to the homeless on the streets of Rome and to support soup kitchens to feed the hungry. "Don't stay behind a desk waiting for people to come to you; get out and search out people in need."

The visit to Sao Paolo for World Youth Day was Francis's first exposure to a mass gathering of young people. During the five-day visit the pope used a small car rather than a motorcade, although many young people were disappointed that they could not see the pope. Francis visited drug rehabilitation centers and the favelas [jersey shacks] of Sao Paolo. He insisted on greeting the poor people personally and was evidently at ease with the young people he encountered. The events culminated with the celebration of Mass on Copacabana beach attended by more than two million people.

It was the pontiff's remarks on the plane back to Rome that gained most attention. Since Pope Paul's first papal flight in 1964, popes regularly addressed the journalists who accompanied them on the plane. During a press conference that lasted almost an hour and a half, the pope answered many questions candidly. He confirmed that the idea of having a committee of eight cardinals came from the College of Cardinals during the meetings prior to the 2013 conclave. When asked about the Institute for Religious Works, he said that he had already begun working on a solution. Francis explained how he learned to be more tolerant, confessing to prejudice regarding the Charismatic Movement. "At the end of the 1970s and the beginning of the 1980s, I had no time for them. Once, speaking about them, I said: 'These people confuse a liturgical celebration with samba lessons!'

I actually said that. Now I regret it. I learned. It is also true that the movement, with good leaders, has made great progress. Now I think that this movement does much good for the church, overall."

He acknowledged the need for greater inclusion of women at all levels of the church's life while ruling out any change in the traditional teaching on women and the priesthood.

Asked about rumors of a "gay lobby" at the Vatican, the pope dismissed these allegations, although he added, "If someone is gay and is searching for the Lord and has good will, then who am I to judge?"

The pope was asked why he did not talk about abortion and same-sex marriage to youth. "The church has already spoken quite clearly on this," he noted. "It was unnecessary to return to it, just as I didn't speak about cheating, lying, or other matters on which the church has a clear teaching."

Although most Italians take their summer vacation in August the pope explained that he had too much to do. In Argentina he never took vacations, preferring to spend time at home and read. In August the pope met with Fr. Antonio Spadero, a fellow Jesuit, and gave Spadero a number of interviews that were published together in *La Civiltà Cattolica* in September. A number of other Jesuit periodicals, including American ones, published the interviews in translation.

Although Francis disliked giving interviews he realized the importance of the format for contemporary audiences. People use phones, magazines, and internet for information, and the interview slips well into this category.

The interview was highly personal and the pope shared a number of ideas and concerns, in particular about his Jesuit formation and his hopes and concerns for the Society of Jesus. He explained how he liked living in the Domus Sanctae Marthae and meeting new people who visited or stayed there. He indicated that governing the church is an enormous task and he said that he adopted the motto attributed to Pope John XXIII, "See everything, turn a blind eye to much, and correct a little."

Despite his optimism, Francis acknowledged that often his first reaction was mistaken. Discernment requires great patience. In particular he reflected on his failures as provincial in Argentina. "'My authoritarian and quick manner of making decisions led me to have serious problems and to be accused of being ultraconservative. I lived a time of great interior crisis when I was in Cordova. To be sure, I have never been like Blessed Imelda [a goody-goody], but I have never been a right-winger. It was my authoritarian way of making decisions that created problems.'" Nonetheless, he affirmed that change is possible in the short term and offered encouragement to those frustrated by the elephantine pace of reform within the church. Rather than a perfect church, Francis hoped for an effective presence in the midst of the people. "I see the Church as a field hospital after battle. It is useless to ask a seriously injured person if he has high cholesterol and about the level of his blood sugars! You have to heal his wounds. Then we can talk about everything else. Heal the wounds, heal the wounds. . . . And you have to start from the ground up."[4]

That spirit of healing was evident in St. Peter's Square when up to one hundred thousand people joined the pope in a four-hour prayer vigil for the war refugees of Syria on the evening of September 8, 2013. A civil war had begun in early 2011 when rebels took part in a political "Arab Spring," an uprising against President Bashar Assad. Within three years 140,000 people had been killed in fighting and up to one-third of the 23 million people had been displaced, fleeing to nearby Turkey, Lebanon, Israel, Egypt, and other countries. It was the first large-scale gesture organized by the pope. It was also his first venture into the fraught area of geopolitics. The pope urged people to seek a solution to the crisis where hundreds of thousands were forced out of their homes.

On September 21 the pope appointed Archbishop Lorenzo Baldisseri as secretary general of the Synod of Bishops. Baldisseri, later to become a cardinal, was given the task of preparing two synods to be held in 2014 and 2015 both with the theme of the family. It was the pope's way to address the requests the cardinals made prior to the conclave to respond to the social challenges of the contemporary family unit.

A day later the pope visited Cagliari on the island of Sardinia where he received a rapturous welcome. The daylong visit included meetings with workers, poor people, prisoners, local leaders, and young people. He listened and offered encouragement, in particular to the youth who struggle with a drug culture and high unemployment.

At the end of September the pope gave an interview to Eugenio Scalfari, founder of the Italian newspaper *La Repubblica*. There was general surprise that a pope would give such an interview, all the greater given that Scalfari was an atheist. However, the interview gave the new pope a forum to express his views on a number of contemporary issues. Francis referred to the deferential court mentality found in the Vatican as "the leprosy of the papacy" that causes a malaise in the universal church. "It sees and looks after the interests of the Vatican, which are still, for the most part, temporal interests. This Vatican-centric view neglects the world around us. I do not share this view and I'll do everything I can to change it. The church is or should go back to being a community of God's people, and priests, pastors and bishops who have the care of souls, are at the service of the people of God."

Francis traveled to the Umbrian town of Assisi on October 4, the feast day of the nation's patron saint. Accompanying him were the eight cardinals of the reform commission who had met in Rome over the previous three days. During his daylong trip the pope spoke about poverty, urging Christians to follow St. Francis's example of stripping themselves to the bare necessities.

"It is unthinkable that a Christian—a true Christian— . . . would want to go down this path of worldliness," Francis told the large crowds gathered in the medieval Room of the Disrobing. "[It] is a homicidal attitude. Spiritual worldliness kills! It kills the soul! It kills the person! it kills the church!" Without divesting themselves of unnecessary wealth, Pope Francis argued, "we would become like Christians in a pastry shop," admiring the beautiful cakes but never receiving true sustenance.[5]

Previously that summer, the pope had also lamented the drowning of some 130 Africans when their boat capsized off the coast of Lampedusa. "The world does not seem to care about those fleeing poverty and hunger in search of freedom but find only death." Rather than be a guest at the table of the Franciscans, the pope hosted a lunch for poor people of the district and spent time with guests with disabilities. The style of pastoral visits had shifted subtly.

Some three thousand people work in the service of the Holy See. At times it appears that the Vatican is the seat of a well-oiled sleek administration. In reality, as Francis often commented, the Vatican is a place that fosters gossip and malicious backbiting that harms the Gospel. Speaking to nuncios gathered at a meeting in June 2013, Pope Francis characteristically advised them to choose new bishops from among the priests who work for the people. "If the priest is very intelligent, let him go off to the university and teach there. He will be better suited there because he should not be a pastor if he does not have the smell of the sheep on him."

The publication of the apostolic exhortation *Evangelii Gaudium*, The Joy of the Gospel, in late November was the first encyclical composed by Francis himself. It was a reflection on the thirteenth assembly of the Synod of Bishops held at the Vatican in October 2013. Written in a conversational style the document was highly different from previous papal documents. The pope's concern for the elderly, the poor, the marginalized, and humans who are trafficked into sexual or economic slavery was evident. But the message was not delivered with pious aspirations for a better world. The message was direct and unflinching. How can we accept a world where a poor person dies and nobody notices while when the stock market loses a couple of cents there is a global outcry? The pope proposed a radical review of the church and the role of Christians in society. One of the greatest needs is not simply to help the poor financially but to help them spiritually. This constitutes real charity and helps them cope with the unevenness of daily life.

While the exhortation generally received good reviews, there were critical voices. American-born Cardinal Raymond Burke, Prefect of the Apostolic Segnatura, the judicial court, noted during an interview with Eternal Word Television Network that the media had distorted the pope's words but that there was a feeling this was partially the pope's fault. Other critics claimed that Francis had a poor grasp of economics, and that without capitalism the poor would never have the opportunity to escape from poverty.

It was now time to replace the secretary of state, the seventy-eight-year-old Cardinal Tarcisio Bertone, who had served under Benedict XVI since 2007. The departure of the cardinal gave Francis the opportunity to appoint a colleague of his own choice: Archbishop Pietro Parolin. Parolin had served as a successful diplomat for many years and was currently the nuncio to Venezuela. He was later added to the advisory council of eight cardinals. During an early December meeting of the council, Cardinal Seán Patrick O'Malley of Boston announced that a special commission concerning the sexual abuse of children by clergy would be established within months. This was to be another priority for the pope.

Prior to the Christmas ceremonies, on December 23, Pope Francis visited his predecessor at Benedict's residence in the Vatican gardens. It was a short and warm exchange. Following his interview with the Jesuit magazine published the previous September, Pope Francis requested the pope emeritus to write a critique and suggestions. To his surprise a few days later a four-page document was delivered via Archbishop Gaenswein. Pope Francis told his sister that he got on well with the previous pope, saying he reminded him of their grandfather, a quiet man but always ready to offer advice.

As the year 2013 ended, the popular impression of Pope Francis was largely positive, particularly in the secular media. *Time* magazine awarded him the accolade of Man of the Year, which had only been accorded to Pope John XXIII and Pope John Paul II.

After the Christmas ceremonies at the Vatican, the pope made a surprise visit to the parish of Sant'Alfonso Maria de' Liguori alla Giustiniana. He had received a letter from some parishioners to visit the church's crib. The crib was unusual in that it featured live animals. Arriving unexpectedly in the evening the pope received a warm welcome. "You are just great!" he told the children. "But so are your parents and grandparents. And don't let me forget the catechists. They have done a very good job teaching you. So, here is my blessing for you but also a blessing for all the babies who are about to be born over the next few days. Let's give them a big welcome!"

Three weeks later the pope visited the parish of Sacred Heart beside Rome's central train station. The visit gave the pope the opportunity of embracing the homeless and migrants who were fed and housed by the diocesan charitable organization. Arriving in his blue Ford Focus hatchback without an escort, the pope explained why he had come. "Cardinal Vallini, the Vicar of Rome, told me about all the help you give the people in need and I wanted to come to see with my own eyes. I am so happy to see what you are doing, the food you are cooking, and the clothes you are sharing."

On February 2, 2014, Pope Francis opened the Year of Consecrated Life. As a religious himself, he understood the charisms of the consecrated life in the church. However, it was a bittersweet opening as two months later the pope confirmed a controversial investigation by the Congregation for the Doctrine of the Faith into the work of the Leadership of Women Religious in America.

The weekly general audiences continued to attract vast crowds to the Vatican each Wednesday. On February 14 Pope Francis welcomed ten thousand engaged couples. To loud laughs he presented them the secret of a happy marriage: "Always ask your partner about what you intend to do. Don't take each other for granted! Believe me, it is better to ask beforehand rather than discover afterward that it lands you in the soup!"

In the early new year Francis extended his reform of the Institute for Religious Works. Four of the five cardinals appointed by Pope Benedict were replaced, as the overseeing body continued to implement changes. Bank accounts that were dormant or suspicious were suspended. Among the suspect accounts were several that investigators believed may have been established to launder money by the Mafia.

The brutal murder of three-year-old Nicola Coco Campolongo, along with his grandfather, Giuseppe Iannicelli, and another twenty-seven-year-old man, shocked Italy. The bodies were discovered in a burnt-out car in Calabria. Although nobody took responsibility for the atrocity, police suspected that the infant's grandfather had been murdered by the local 'Ndrangheta crime organization. The child's twenty-four-year-old mother was in jail for selling illegal drugs.

Pope Francis roundly condemned the killers. "This violence against such a small child seems without precedent in the history of crime," the pope said some days later. "Let us pray with Coco, who is certainly with Jesus in heaven, and for the people who carried out this crime, so that they repent and convert to the Lord."

On February 22 Francis summoned the cardinals to Rome to discuss care of the family, and during a ceremony held at St. Peter's, nineteen new cardinals were created. Rather than creating cardinals in the traditional sees, such as Venice, the pope chose candidates from poor countries such as Haiti and Burkino Faso, underlining his desire to expand the church into the impoverished areas of the world. The ceremony was the first occasion when Benedict XVI appeared in public with Pope Francis. Shortly after the meeting with the cardinals the pope published a document setting up a new economic prefecture to reorganize the finances of the Vatican and appointed Australia's Cardinal George Pell the first prefect. The Institute for Religious Works was to be retained, although in a greatly reduced form. As the new prefect observed, poverty does not imply carelessness with other people's money, and donations are to be invested wisely so that they can contribute to alleviation of human suffering.

The first anniversary of Francis's election on March 13 offered the opportunity to reflect on the impact of the pontificate. While the pope wanted no celebrations, media observers noted the seismic changes that had engulfed the church over the previous twelve months.

The pope's concern for victims of organized crime in Italy was expressed on March 21 when he attended a prayer vigil for victims of the Mafia. Some seven hundred people crowded into the Church of San Gregory the Great, close to the Vatican, to pray for peace. The pope listened solemnly as the names of the victims were read out. Francis was determined to tackle the problem of church collaboration with criminal bosses in the south of Italy.

Many people are astonished that the Vatican has retained so much artwork and treasures from a former age. Pope Francis repeatedly stated how much he wanted a church that would care for the poor and would be poor itself. Was it not time to divest itself of some of the traditions that belonged to a bygone age? Suggestions were made to sell off the Vatican museums and other real estate. The issue was too vast to be decided quickly, but the pope decided that the gardens of Castelgandolfo should be opened to the public to defray the cost of their maintenance. He reserved a decision for the future of the now disused villa.

The issue of episcopal residences attracted global attention. Many bishops resided in sumptuous residences while the pope lived in a three-room suite in the Domus Sanctae Marthae. In October 2013 Bishop Franz-Peter Tebartz-van Elst of the German diocese of Limburg was suspended for spending thirty-one million euros (40 million dollars) on his residence. Six months later he was replaced by a new administrator. Shortly afterward Archbishop Wilton Gregory of Atlanta was forced to apologize for spending more than two million dollars on a new residence that he later sold. It was part of the "Francis effect."

According to Bishop Marcelo Sánchez Sorondo, Chancellor of the Pontifical Academies of Sciences and Social Sciences, two passions dominated Pope Francis's program: the end of human trafficking and creating respect and harmony between Christians and other faiths. On March 17 representatives of the archbishop of Canterbury, the grand mufti of Al Azhar in Egypt, and the pope signed a declaration with the New Global Network to help end the enslavement of upward of twenty-nine million victims of human trafficking.

While Francis had carefully avoided an involvement in Argentinian politics he was obliged to receive President Cristina Kirchner on her visit to Rome. As archbishop of Buenos Aires Cardinal Bergoglio had reportedly requested a meeting with the president seven times since her election in 2007, and each time he had been refused. Kirchner had also absented herself on July 9 for the *Te Deum* ceremony at the cathedral in Buenos Aires that marked Independence Day. While the pope and president posed for photographs before lunch at the Domus Sanctae Marthae, they could not hide their discomfort. The two had clashed over issues of morality in Argentina, and Pope Francis wanted to avoid appearing to support Kirchner's bid for a third-term reelection.

During the funeral of Pope John Paul II some in the crowd waved banners inscribed with the words *Santo Subito*—make him a saint immediately. Throughout his twenty-six-year pontificate the Polish pope had courted fierce controversy both within and without the church. Few however could contest his undoubted holiness. Only five years following John Paul's death Pope Benedict had beatified him at a colorful ceremony, attended by half a million pilgrims packed into St. Peter's Square and its environs. In agreeing to canonize the Polish pontiff, Francis decided on a joint ceremony where Pope John XXIII, beatified in 2000, would also be canonized. Francis may have intended to bridge a gap between progressives, who championed John XXIII and the Second Vatican Council, and the conservatives, who promoted John Paul II as a defender of orthodoxy. Although this simplistic view prevailed among Catholics, Francis hoped to balance both streams within the church.

On April 27 in St. Peter's Square, Pope Francis presided over the historic ceremony attended by 1,000 bishops, 160 cardinals, emeritus Pope Benedict, and close to 1 million faithful. Media commentators observed that Francis's style was very much that of John XXIII, noted for his smile and his love of contact with people and his down-to-earth simplicity.

Although no pope had visited the Holy Land until Paul VI's historic visit in 1964, Pope John Paul II and Pope Benedict XVI had made successful visits to the region. Pope Francis accepted the invitation of the Israeli, Jordanian, and Palestinian authorities to visit the Holy Land in late May. Given the serious humanitarian crisis in nearby Syria, the proposed journey was fraught with difficulties. To assist him, the pope invited Rabbi Abraham Skorka and a professor of Islamic studies, Omar Abboud, old friends from Argentina who both accompanied him on the journey.

The pastoral visit began in Jordan on May 24 where the pope celebrated Mass at a stadium in Amman before meeting disabled people and refugees. On the second day, while on his way to Israel, the pope stopped at a wall in Bethlehem separating Israel from the West Bank. The pope had spent the morning in Bethlehem where he had listened to the laments of Palestinians who bemoaned their treatment at the hands of Israelis. The vigil and fast for Syria called for by Pope Francis the previous September was recalled with gratitude by the Palestinians, both Christian and Muslim alike. Every move the pontiff made was monitored. Many Israelis were offended that Pope Francis seemed to approve of the Palestinian Authority, which the Holy See had supported for several years. By placing his hand on the dividing wall he anticipated the gesture he would make the next day at the Wailing Wall in Jerusalem.

Arriving in Jerusalem that evening the pope took part in a moving ecumenical meeting with the patriarch of Constantinople, Bartholomew I, regarded by Orthodox Christians as the figurehead for all Christendom much as Catholics regard the bishop of Rome. Just fifty years earlier Pope Paul VI and Patriarch Athenagoras had similarly met in Jerusalem and rescinded mutual decrees of excommunication that dated from a dispute between the papacy and patriarchate in the eleventh century. Patriarch Bartholomew had made history by attending Pope Francis's inauguration in Rome in 2013, the first patriarch in modern times to do so. Francis and Bartholomew agreed to lay the groundwork for an ecumenical synod to take place in Nicea in 2025, the 1700th anniversary of the First Council of Nicea.[6] The announcement gave new impetus to ecumenical dialogue between the two churches.

The following morning the pope paid a visit to the Wailing Wall where he inserted a paper on which was written the Our Father into a crack in the wall. After the pope's moment of silent prayer, Skorka and Abboud stepped up to him and the three locked in an embrace. "We did it!" Rabbi Skorka whispered delightedly into their ears. Later that morning the entourage traveled to the Holocaust memorial at Yad Vashim, where the pope met survivors of the Second World War and kissed their hands. The day included visits to the Israel authorities and Mass in the Upper Cenacle where, according to tradition, the Last Supper was observed by Jesus and his apostles. In particular the pope appealed for the end of the exodus of Christians from the Holy Land.

The issue of peace was uppermost in Francis's mind, and prior to his departure he invited the president of Israel, Shimon Peres, and the president of the Palestinian Authority, Mahoud Abbas, to join him in the Vatican to pray for peace. To his delight both leaders accepted the invitation. Two weeks later, at the beginning of June, the pope welcomed both visitors to his home at the Domus Sanctae Marthae before going into the nearby Vatican gardens where each was invited to pray for peace. Although not necessarily religious men, the two politicians nonetheless summed up the hopes and aspirations of their nations for an end to hostility.

A clue to the mind of Francis is found in the choice of pastoral visits. Invitations from all over the world arrive almost daily at the Vatican. Within Italy the pope visited places that had social problems. The visits to the parishes of Rome were almost always to the peripheries.

Although previous popes such as John Paul II and Benedict had forcibly condemned the various crime gangs that plagued Italy, their words seemed to have little effect. An Austrian priest had been excommunicated for his support of the ordination of women, same-sex marriage, and divorced and remarried couples who are barred from receiving communion. Yet those who belonged to the Mafia, the 'Ndrangheta, and Cosa Nostra criminal gangs were not excommunicated and in some cases their activity condoned. These criminals adopted Catholic religious imagery and even the festivities surrounding the annual celebration of a town's patron saint was regularly an opportunity for un-scrupulous thugs to extort money from local businesses. Some clergy came from established Mafia families. Successive Italian governments had been unable to put an end to the illegal activities and some politicians had taken Mafia help and money to obtain election.

During a visit to the southern Diocese of Cassano all' Ionio on June 24 where a three-year-old child had been murdered, Pope Francis preached an impassioned homily, condemning the cowardice of those engaged in corrupt criminal organizations. "The 'Ndrangheta is simply this—the adoration of evil and contempt of the common good," adding in the clearest terms, "Mafiosi are excommunicated."

These themes were taken up again during a visit to Caserta on Saturday, July 26, where Francis urged the citizens not to engage in criminal activity. The area had been polluted by illegal dumping of toxic materials that threatened not just the citizens of the region but of Italy and neighboring countries. The pope was aware that his words could do little more than challenge, but his very presence encouraged his listeners to think how they could contribute positively to change.

One of the greatest plagues of the contemporary church was the sexual abuse of children and its mishandling by bishops. The centuries-old issue, which had been long suppressed, had exploded in the media in the late 1990s. Catholics and non-Catholics alike were disgusted at the sordid revelations. What infuriated most was the way in which many church authorities had covered up abusive clerics and virtually ignored the victims who had to live with the stigma of abuse into their adulthood. The Holy See had been slow in responding and had been severely criticized by the United Nations. In early May the newly established Pontifical Commission for the Protection of Minors met for the first time. The eight-member committee, led by Cardinal Seán Patrick O'Malley, included civil and canon lawyers and mental health experts. Among the founding members was Irishwoman Marie Collins, who had been sexually abused by a priest at the age of thirteen. For decades she had been an eloquent voice in calling for proper recognition of the criminal mismanagement of many bishops and demanded adequate recompense for the victims. When Pope Francis welcomed the team to the Domus Sanctae Marthae, he asked them to draw from their wide expertise when writing the statutes. In addition, the committee was given the possibility of expansion to include members from different parts of the world.

By fifteen months into his pontificate, Francis had not yet met formally with a group of survivors of clerical sexual abuse. In early July he invited six survivors to stay at the Domus Sanctae Marthae. On the night the six with their supporters arrived, they had dinner in the refectory. The pope welcomed them and confirmed that they would celebrate Mass with him the next morning. Rather than invite a large group the decision was made to limit this meeting to six so that the pope could spend time with them.

During the homily the following morning, the pope asked forgiveness for the manner in which the church had betrayed their trust. He identified child abuse as both a crime and a sin and acknowledged that shame was sometimes compounded by the suicide of victims. The homily was not addressed only to those in the chapel but to victims worldwide. "You and all those who were abused by clergy are loved by God. I pray that the remnants of the darkness that touched you may be healed by the embrace of the Child Jesus and that the harm that was done to you will give way to renewed faith and joy." For the rest of the morning he spent half an hour with each individual, listening to his and her stories.

"It is better that I listen rather than talk," he explained as he began each encounter.

The pope's penchant for granting interviews caused headaches for the press office. Following the third interview, granted to Eugenio Scalfari, founder of the Italian daily newspaper *La Repubblica,* the press office found itself in the eye of a media storm. Fr. Lombardi had the delicate task of explaining to reporters that the account of the interview with the ninety-year-old journalist was done without notes or a recording, and the press officer seemed to contradict the account of what the pope had said.

Given the controversy following the first interview, Vatican officials were perplexed as to why Francis would agree to another. Some were irritated that the pope chose to speak to journalists about sensitive issues such as child sexual abuse, celibacy, and remarriage. In April a woman in Argentina claimed that the pope had telephoned her in response to a letter she had written and said that the pope had assured her that her divorced and remarried husband could receive Holy Communion. Lombardi was regularly obliged to issue clarifications about phone calls of which the content ought to have been private. However, since April there were no more stories about phone calls so Lombardi may have succeeded in convincing the pope to refrain from random calls.

The issue of celibacy caused the greatest debate in the interview with Scalfari. Although the pope expressed his personal appreciation of the law of obligatory celibacy for priests, he acknowledged that the law in the Latin Church dated from the eleventh century. Prior to that, clerical celibacy was optional. The Eastern Catholic Church allows married clergy, and Francis indicated that the issue would be looked at region by region. According to Scalfari the pope had remarked, "There are solutions and I will find them."

During meetings with some bishops the pope expressed several times an openness to discuss the issue that previous popes had refused to countenance. When Bishop Erwin Kräutler of Xingu, Brazil, originally from Austria, met with the pope in April 2014 the bishop told him of the practical difficulties celibacy caused in finding candidates for the priesthood. In an interview with the Austrian newspaper *Die Presse* the bishop said that the two had discussed the situation in the Amazon where, due to the lack of priests, only 10 percent of the people could attend weekly Mass. Bishop Kräutler, quoting the pope, stated that Francis asked bishops in regional conferences "to make bold and courageous suggestions." This was not a way of sidestepping the issue but of granting more autonomy to local conferences. During his time as bishop in Argentina, Bergoglio had often criticized the centralized bureaucracy of the Vatican.

On the related but distinct issue of the ordination of women to the priesthood, the pope stood firmly by the tradition of the church that the sacrament can only be conferred on men.

As Pope Benedict XVI had indicated his intention to travel to Brazil to celebrate World Youth Day in July 2013, Pope Francis simply fulfilled his predecessor's promise. The impending retirement of President Perez of Israel had impelled Pope Francis to make the May trip to the Holy Land. But the first major trip entirely of Francis's choice was to Asia, in particular to South Korea.

As a young Jesuit, Jorge Bergoglio had hoped to be assigned to the missions in Japan. Delicate health had determined that his superiors retain him in Argentina. In August 2014 the pope left Rome for a five-day visit to Asia. Ostensibly the occasion was to take part in the regional Youth Festival. Catholics count for only 10 percent of the population but the church had experienced sudden growth in recent years. Koreans learned about Christianity through the writings of the seventeenth-century Jesuit missionary to China, Fr. Matteo Ricci, but the faith was spread by people, not Western missionaries.

In 2001 there were 44,446 priests in Asia, but by 2011 that number had risen to 60,042. During the same period the number of priests in Europe declined from 206,761 to 186,489. In a period of fifty years, membership of the Catholic Church in South Korea rose from 1 percent to 10 percent in 2014.

At a ceremony in Gwanghwamun Square, Francis beatified 124 martyrs who died in the eighteenth and nineteenth centuries. "They challenge us to think what, if anything, we would be prepared to die for," he said during the ceremony. It was in that square that many of the founders of Christianity in Korea were beheaded.

The pope insisted on driving in a simple car, spurning an elaborate motorcade in this image-conscious country. His meeting with young people was successful, as evidenced by the number of requests to pose for photographs. "Oh my English is very, very poor," he lamented before ad-libbing in Italian to the delighted youths. At the final Mass the pope called for North and South Korea, both locked into a Cold War since 1950, to find peaceful means to coexist.

On his return to Rome from South Korea Pope Francis received the tragic news that his nephew's wife and two children had been killed in a horrific car crash in Córdoba in Argentina. His nephew, Emanuel Horacio Bergoglio, had survived but his wife Valeria died along with their eight-month-old infant, José, and his two-year-old brother, Antonio.

Francis was deeply shocked by the fatal accident. There was no possibility of his returning for the funerals, and he had to content himself with frequent phone calls to various members of his family.

During a visit on 13 September to the war memorial of Redipuglia near the Italian–Slovenian border to mark the centenary of the outbreak of the First World War, Pope Francis recalled members of his own family who had enlisted in the army during those years—in particular his grandfather Giovanni, who had fought in the military trenches near the Isonzo River. For Francis there was little heroic about war but he praised the soldiers who were forced into hostilities in the effort to defend their homeland.

During his homily at Mass near the cemetery, Francis grimly warned that World War III had already broken out in part. "War is irrational; its only plan is to bring destruction: it seeks to grow by destroying. Greed, intolerance, the lust for power. These motives underlie the decision to go to war and they are too often justified by an ideology," he told the thousands who huddled under umbrellas to shelter from the incessant rain.

Within a month of his South Korean visit Pope Francis made a daylong visit to Albania. The eleven-hour trip on September 21, 2014, was the pontiff's first European visit. In 1967 the dictator Enver Hoxha had declared Albania to be the first atheistic state and adherents of many faiths suffered persecution or execution. Francis met victims and encouraged both Catholics and members of other faiths to make use of their renewed religious freedom. His choice of a country on Europe's periphery—rather than in its traditional Catholic heartland—was eloquent.

The human family has been the theme of the pontiff's greatest project to date. In October 2013 the Pope had announced that an "extraordinary synod" would be held in the Vatican in October 2014, ahead of the regular Synod of Bishops scheduled for 2015. Pope Francis prepared for the synod by celebrating the weddings of twenty couples from the Diocese of Rome on September 15, 2014. One of the brides was already a mother, some of the couples had been married before, and some had been separated. The Pope clearly wanted to show his pastoral care for couples in irregular unions.

The theme of such unions was to reoccur during the Synod held at the Vatican October 5–19, 2014. Prior to its opening, the pontiff called for frank discussion. He may have gotten more than he bargained for when a group of cardinals contributed to a book that resolutely challenged modification to the church's teaching on doctrinal issues. Some saw this as a subtle challenge to Francis's "mission of mercy."[7]

The synod was a forum for frank debate and discussion, contrasting with previous synods that had been controlled by a curial agenda. Francis introduced an air of liberty but not all were pleased. Some complained that the pope was sowing uncertainty and confusion in the minds of people.

There was some truth in this, however. Halfway through the three-week synod an interim document spoke warmly about people with homosexual desires and those in broken marriages. Many bishops wanted to reach out and change the language hitherto used in describing such issues, in order to provide a more pastoral approach. Fresh in the bishops' memories was a 1986 letter from the Congregation for the Doctrine of the Faith, signed by Cardinal Joseph Ratzinger, in which homosexuality was described as "a more or less strong tendency ordered toward an intrinsic moral evil."[8] While the interim document spoke of the gifts and qualities of homosexual people, the final *Relatio Synodi* simply observed that "men and women with a homosexual tendency ought to be received with respect and sensitivity."

An Australian couple, Ron and Mavis Pirola had been invited as some of the married observers to the synod. In straightforward language they told the bishops that many church statements on the family were "from another plant" and "not terribly relevant" to the lives of ordinary people. Such candor was rare in the synod hall and took several bishops by surprise.

The similarly cool reception of the 180 bishops to the admittance to Holy Communion of divorced couples disappointed many Catholics, yet Pope Francis was in an upbeat mood when he addressed the bishops at the conclusion. "Personally I would be very worried and saddened if it were not for . . . these animated discussions; . . . if all were in a state of agreement, or silent in a false and quietist peace," he said in off-the-cuff remarks. Yet many were dismayed when the conservative Cardinal Raymond Burke, Prefect of the Supreme Tribunal of the Apostolic Signatura (the church's court of law) and one of the contributors to the book defending current doctrine on the eve of the synod, was transferred to the office of Patron of the Knights of the Order of Malta, a position that some perceive as merely ceremonial, with very little actual responsibility.

As the pontificate unrolled, Francis developed a sharp sense of political acumen. During an insightful address to the European parliament the pope both praised and chided the assembled politicians. The speech, interrupted fourteen times by applause, received a standing ovation.

As a Latin American pope, Francis has used his knowledge of the Hispanic world to foster peace in troubled spots. In Colombia he encouraged the government and rebels to dialogue and urged Mexican drug barons to abandon violence, extortion, and mass killings. While his appeals for peace in the Middle East appeared to falter, Francis contributed to the successful normalizing of diplomatic relations between Cuba and the United States, which had stalled for half a century. During his meeting with President Barack Obama in March 2014, Francis appealed to the American leader to dialogue with the Cuban president, Raúl Castro. In October of that same year ambassadors of both nations met with Francis, and two months later relations were normalized.

Those who know Jorge Bergoglio well are aware of his tenacious personality. In the early days of his papacy Francis seemed to be a "white caped crusader," helping the poor and mortifying the rich. This simplification is by no means accurate; Bergoglio has always been a divisive character, and people side either with him or against him. While he retains his popularity among rank-and-file Catholics, his legacy will require even more substantial change. The problems, challenges, and opportunities at the dawn of the third Christian millennium are daunting. The first two years of the pontificate were filled with both hope and frustration. The personal challenge for Pope Francis will be to retain the momentum, uniting people who share his vision of offering Jesus to the contemporary world.

Notes

Chapter One: Beginnings—pages 1–12

1. Francesca Ambrogetti and Sergio Rubin, *Pope Francis: Conversations with Jorge Bergoglio* (New York: G. P. Putnam's Sons, 2013), 34.

Chapter Two: The Society of Jesus—pages 13–29

1. Gustavo Gutierrez, "Memory and Prophecy," in *The Option for the Poor in Christian Theology*, ed. Daniel G. Groody (Notre Dame, IN: University of Notre Dame Press, 2007), 25.

2. Saint John Paul II, Speech to the Third General Conference of the Latin American Episcopate (Puebla, Mexico, January 28, 1979), I.4.

3. Additional Statement by Father Franz Jalics, SJ, March 20, 2013, http://www.jesuiten.org/aktuelles/details/article/erganzende-erklarung-von-pater-franz-jalics-sj.html.

4. Ambrogetti and Rubin, *Pope Francis*, 200.

Chapter Three: Bishop of Buenos Aires—pages 30–63

1. Ambrogetti and Rubin, *Pope Francis*, 163.

2. Stefania Falasca, "Quello che avrei detto al concistoro," *30 Giorni* (November 2007), http://www.30giorni.it/articoli_id_15978_11.htm.

3. Blessed Pope Paul VI, Encyclical on the Development of Peoples (*Populorum Progressio*), March 26, 1967, 23.

4. Jorge Mario Bergoglio and Abraham Skorka, *On Heaven and Earth: Pope Francis on Faith, Family and the Church in the 21st Century* (New York: Image, 2013), 50–51.

Chapter Four: The First Conclave—pages 64–68

1. Cardinal Joseph Ratzinger, Homily to the College of Cardinals (Vatican Basilica, April 18, 2005), http://www.vatican.va/gpII /documents/homily-pro-eligendo-pontifice_20050418_en.html.

Chapter Six: The Abdication—pages 74–83

1. Pope Benedict XVI, Declaratio (February 10, 2013), http://www .vatican.va/holy_father/benedict_xvi/speeches/2013/february /documents/hf_ben-xvi_spe_20130211_declaratio_en.html.

2. Pope Emeritus Benedict XVI, Greeting to the Faithful of the Diocese of Albano (Castel Gandolfo, February 28, 2013), http://www .vatican.va/holy_father/benedict_xvi/speeches/2013/february /documents/hf_ben-xvi_spe_20130228_fedeli-albano_en.html.

3. See "Bergoglio's Intervention: A diagnosis of the problems in the Church," *Vatican Radio* (March 27, 2013), http://en.radiovaticana .va/storico/2013/03/27/bergoglios_intervention_a_diagnosis_of_the _problems_in_the_church/en1-677269.

Chapter Eight: A Pontificate Begins—pages 93–136

1. Pope Francis, Homily for the Fifth Sunday of Lent (Vatican, March 17, 2013), http://w2.vatican.va/content/francesco/en /homilies/2013/documents/papa-francesco_20130317_omelia-santa -anna.html.

2. Pope Francis, Homily for the Chrism Mass (St. Peter's Basilica, March 28, 2013), http://w2.vatican.va/content/francesco/en /homilies/2013/documents/papa-francesco_20130328_messa -crismale.html.

3. Fabiano Frayssinet, "Lo que interesa no es Bergoglio y su pasado, sino Francisco y su future," Inter Press Service, March 18, 2013,

http://www.ipsnoticias.net/2013/03/lo-que-interesa-no-es-bergoglio
-y-su-pasado-sino-francisco-y-su-futuro.

4. Antonio Spadaro, SJ, "A Big Heart Open to God: The exclusive interview with Pope Francis," *America,* September 30, 2013, http://www.americamagazine.org/pope-interview.

5. Pope Francis, "Meeting with the Poor Assisted by Caritas" (Assisi, Italy, October 4, 2013), http://w2.vatican.va/content/francesco/en/speeches/2013/october/documents/papa-francesco_20131004_poveri-assisi.html.

6. Nat da Polis, "Bartholomew: With Francis, we invite all Christians to celebrate the first synod of Nicaea in 2025," *AsiaNews,* May 29, 2014, http://www.asianews.it/news-en/Bartholomew-:-With-Francis,-we-invite-all-Christians-to-celebrate-the-first-synod-of-Nicaea-in-2025-31213.html.

7. Robert Dodaro, ed., *Remaining in the Truth of Christ: Marriage and Communion in the Catholic Church* (San Francisco: Ignatius, 2014).

8. Congregation for the Doctrine of the Faith, Letter to the Bishops of the Catholic Church on the Pastoral Care of Homosexual Persons, October 1, 1986, 3.

Index

Abboud, Omar, 125, 126
Albania, 133
Aramburo, Juan Carlos
  (archbishop), 25, 46
Argentina, 54, 89; civil unrest
  in, 21–23, 34; Córdoba, 12,
  29, 116, 132; emigration to,
  1, 3–5; politics in, 23, 34,
  43–44, 46–47, 48–50, 61, 63,
  124; San Miguel, 19, 28. *See
  also* Buenos Aires; Dirty War
Argentinians: and Cardinal
  Bergoglio, 40; and Pope
  Francis, 97, 98–99, 102
Arrupe, Pedro, 16, 20
Athenagoras (patriarch), 99, 126

Baldisseri, Lorenzo (cardinal),
  117
baptism, 2, 6, 48, 58–59
Bartholomew I (patriarch), 65,
  99, 126
Becciu, Giovanni (archbishop),
  104
Benedict XVI (pope), 53, 54,
  55, 67, 68, 69–72, 82, 93,
100, 107, 111, 121, 125, 127,
  131, 134; and Francis, 54,
  56, 62, 88, 100–101, 120,
  122; resignation/retirement
  of, 1, 72, 74–78; and Vatican
  leaks scandal, 71–72, 101–2,
  109
Bergoglio family, 1–12, 18, 31,
  37, 95, 112, 132, 133
Bergoglio, Alberto Horacio
  (brother), 6, 8, 112
Bergoglio, Bishop: appointment
  of, 30–31; financial
  administration of, 39–40;
  role as, 33–40. *See also under*
  clergy
Bergoglio, Cardinal:
  appointment of, 40–41; and
  retirement, 72–73; role as,
  42–45, 47–63, 75–76, 80. *See
  also under* clergy
Bergoglio, Giovanni
  (grandfather), 1, 2–5, 38, 133
Bergoglio, Giovanni Mario
  (father), 1, 2, 3, 5–6, 7, 8–9,
  10, 12, 41

Bergoglio, María Elena (sister), 8, 40, 41, 112, 120

Bergoglio, Marta Regina (sister), 8, 112

Bergoglio, Oscar Adrian (brother), 8

Bergoglio, Rosa Vasallo de (grandmother), 2–5, 6, 7, 38

Bertello, Giuseppe, 110

Bertone, Tarcisio (cardinal), 72, 119

bishop. *See* Bergoglio, Bishop

bishops: conferences of, 24–25, 53, 54, 62, 131; documents by, 24, 45–46, 57–58, 134; synods of, 42–43, 117, 119, 133–35. *See also* Vatican II

Brazil, 53, 82, 102, 108, 131

Buenos Aires, 34; Diocese of, 32, 33–40, 44–52, 60–63; Flores, 5–6, 34, 56, 73; history of, 5, 32–33; Ramos Mejía, 7, 60

Buenos Aires Metropolitan Cathedral, 31

Burke, Raymond (cardinal), 119, 135

Calabresi, Ubaldo (archbishop), 30–31

capitalism, 21, 54, 119

cardinal. *See* Bergoglio, Cardinal

Careaga, Esther Balarino de, 9

Caribbean, the, 23, 109

Castellano, Ramón José (archbishop), 18

Castro, Raúl (president), 136

catechists, 51, 120

Catholic Action, 2–3, 9

celibacy, 19, 59–60, 69, 110, 130–31

Charismatic Movement, 114–15

children. *See* youth and Pope Francis

Chile, 12, 17, 54

China, 16, 111, 131

Christian unity, 53, 54–55

Clement XIV (pope), 16, 95

clergy: and Bishop Bergoglio, 35–36, 38–39, 104; and Cardinal Bergoglio, 42–43, 44–45, 47–49, 50, 60–61, 62–63; and Pope Francis, 95–96, 103, 104–5, 107–8, 111, 113–14, 118–19, 122, 123–24

Cold War, 19, 21, 132

Colegio de la Immaculada, Santa Fé, 18

Colegio del Salvador, Buenos Aires, 18

Colegio Del Salvador, Córdoba, 29

Colegio Máximo de San José, 20, 21, 27, 29

Colombia, 54, 81, 135; Medellín, 24

Communion and Liberation (religious group), 16, 28, 82

Communism, 9, 21, 22, 25, 65

confession, 10, 29, 48, 50, 92, 105

Congregation for the Doctrine of the Faith, 54, 69, 121, 134

Cuba, 135–36

Del Regno, Daniel, 97
de Roucy, Thierry, 35
Di Paola, José María "Pepe," 51
Dirty War, 21–23, 25–27, 46,
    48–50, 62–63, 111–12
divorce/remarriage, 60–61, 127,
    130, 134, 135
Dolan, Timothy (cardinal), 77, 82
Domus Sanctae Marthae, 93, 96,
    99–100, 103, 106, 107, 108,
    115, 123, 124, 127, 129
Donatis, Don Angelo, 104–5
drug addiction/industry, 46, 50–
    51, 52, 96, 114, 117, 122

Eastern Rite, 37, 130
education, Bergoglio's, 7, 9, 11,
    17, 18, 28, 29
Egan, Edward (cardinal), 42
emigration. *See under* Argentina
encyclicals of Francis, 111, 119
evangelicalism, 53, 111

family challenges, 58, 60–61,
    117, 130, 133–35
Fascism, 3, 22
Feroci, Enrico, 105
financial administration of
    Francis, 110–11, 114, 121,
    122–24
football club, San Lorenzo, 8, 99
Francis of Assisi, 89, 94–95, 118

Gaenswein, Georg (archbishop),
    71, 77, 100, 113, 120

general audiences, 103–4, 106–
    7, 121
Germany, 28–29, 56, 69, 70
Giussani, Don Luigi, 28, 82
Gracias, Oswald, 110
Gregory, Wilton (archbishop),
    124
Guardini, Romano, 28
Gutiérrez, Gustavo, 23

health of Bergoglio/Francis, 10,
    108, 131
Holy Land, 97, 125–26, 131
homosexuality, 115, 134. *See
    also* same-sex marriage
human rights. *See* social justice
Hummes, Cláudio (cardinal),
    75–76, 91, 94

Ignatius of Loyola, 13–16, 17
Institute for Religious Works,
    82, 114, 121, 122
Institute of Sankt Georg,
    Frankfurt, 29
interviews of Francis, 33, 36,
    44–45, 58–59, 103, 115–16,
    117, 120, 129–30. *See also*
    media
Ireland, 28, 62, 71
Israel, 116, 125–26, 131
Italians and Pope Francis, 89,
    90, 103
Italy, 3–4, 5, 7, 41, 82, 108,
    122–23, 127, 128; Asti, 1, 2;
    Castelgandolfo, 76, 77, 88,
    100–101, 123; Lampedusa,
    113, 118; Portacomaro, 41;

Sardegna/Sardinia, 32, 117; Turin, 2, 3, 6, 41. *See also* Rome

Jalics, Francisco, 25–27
Japan, 11, 16, 131
Jerusalem, 99, 102, 126
Jesuit Order, history of, 13–17
Jesuit Order and Bergoglio/Francis: vocation in, 12, 17–18, 19–20, 27–29; as provincial of, 20–21, 25–27, 47, 104, 116; as bishop, 34; as pope, 96
Jewish-Catholic relations, 55–56, 57, 59, 70, 97–98, 102, 125–27
John Paul II (pope), 16, 24–25, 31, 37, 42, 43, 64–67, 69, 70, 75, 78, 81, 93, 100, 107, 109, 120, 124–25, 127
John XXIII (pope), 18, 70, 116, 120, 125
Jordan, 125

Kirchner, Cristina (president), 124
Kirchner, Néstor (president), 43–44, 57
Krajewski, Konrad (bishop), 114
Kräutler, Erwin (bishop), 131

Laghi, Pio (archbishop), 50
Latino, 89, 107, 111, 112
liberation theology, 23, 25, 45, 54, 112

Lombardi, Federico, 79, 130
López Trujillo, Alfonso (bishop), 24, 25

Mafia, 122, 123, 127–28
Maradiaga, Óscar Andrés Rodríguez, 110
Marcó, Guillermo, 40–41
marriage, 121. *See also* divorce/remarriage; same-sex marriage
Martini, Carlo (cardinal), 68
Marx, Reinhard, 110
Marxism, 22, 24, 27, 46, 54
Mass, celebration of, 44, 48, 52, 61, 95–96, 98–99, 100, 103, 104, 105, 106, 108, 113, 114, 125, 129
media, 40, 59, 68, 72, 81–82, 90–91, 92–93, 95, 119, 120, 123, 125, 128, 130; press conferences, 79, 114–15. *See also* interviews
Menem, Carlos (president), 43, 57
Mexico, 53–54, 108, 135; Puebla, 24
Mugica, Carlos, 48–49
Muslim-Catholic relations, 56–57, 70–71, 105, 113, 124, 125–27
Mussolini, Benito, 3, 7

Nicolás, Adolfo, 96–97
Nicea, 126

Obama, Barack (president), 135–36

O'Farrell, Richard, 20, 21
Ogñénovich, Emilio (bishop), 31
O'Malley, Seán Patrick
    (cardinal), 79, 81–82, 110,
    120, 129
Ortega, Jaime (cardinal), 80
Orthodox church, 54–55
Ossa, Francisco Javier
    Errázuriz, 110
Ouellet, Marc (cardinal), 81

Palestine, 125, 126–27
Pallotine victims, 49–50
Parolin, Pietro (archbishop),
    120
Pasinya, Laurent Monsengwo,
    110
Paul VI (pope), 19, 45, 99, 107,
    110, 125, 126
Pell, George (cardinal), 110, 122
Perón, Isabel (president), 22, 48
Perón, Juan (president), 22
personality of Bergoglio/Francis,
    18, 19, 21, 26, 43, 44–45, 59,
    61–62, 95–96, 97, 112, 116,
    125, 136; frugality/simplicity,
    20, 34, 36, 37–38, 40–41, 85–
    86, 90, 93, 99, 103, 107, 114,
    118, 125, 132; generosity, 27,
    52–53, 58–59, 100, 105, 106,
    113–14; humility, 37, 51–52,
    53, 55, 59, 61, 87, 90, 91, 92,
    101; sense of humor, 41, 42,
    59, 62, 93, 95, 99, 103, 121
Podestá, Jerónimo, 60–61
Poli, Mario Aurelio (cardinal),
    109

politics and Bergoglio/Francis,
    43–44, 50, 57, 63, 116–17,
    124, 126–27, 135–36
poor, 23–24; Bergoglio's
    support of the, 27, 33, 35,
    40, 43, 47, 52, 55, 57, 61;
    Francis's support of the, 94,
    99, 105, 114, 117, 118, 119,
    122; Jesuits' support of the,
    16–17, 20, 21, 27; and
    Movement of Priests for the
    Third World, 45–46, 47, 49
pope, election process/conclave
    for, 64, 66–68, 75, 76, 78–83,
    84–86, 103, 114; Francis's,
    84–91
poverty. *See* poor
Pozzoli, Enrique, 6
preaching/homilies, 44, 52, 54,
    61–62, 95, 100, 102, 104,
    106, 109, 128, 129, 133. *See
    also* speeches
priest (Bergoglio): decision to
    become a, 10; ordained as a,
    18; role as a, 28, 29
priests, assassinations of, 17,
    48–50
priests and Francis. *See* clergy
Priests for the Third World, 45–
    46, 47, 49
prison ministry, 52, 117
pro-life, 19, 54, 57–58, 98, 115
public, the, and Francis, 89–90,
    92, 95, 96, 100, 102, 103–4,
    105–7, 108, 112–13, 114–15,
    116–18, 120–21, 123, 125–
    27, 132, 133

Quarracino, Antonio (cardinal), 31, 36–37, 39

Ratzinger, Joseph (cardinal). *See* Benedict XVI (pope)
reconciliation. *See* confession
Reformation, 14, 15–16
remarriage. *See* divorce/remarriage
Roman Curia, 70, 79, 82, 110
Rome, 20, 37, 40–41, 75–76, 78, 88, 97–98, 99, 103, 106, 108, 109, 127. *See also* Vatican
Romero, Oscar (archbishop), 112

Salesians, 6–7, 8, 11
same-sex marriage, 63, 115, 127
Sánchez, Sergio, 99
Sánchez Sorondo, Marcelo (archbishop), 99, 124
Sandri, Leonardo (cardinal), 64, 99
San José de Flores church, 10
San José de San Miguel church, 28
San José Seminary, 18
San Lorenzo football club, 8, 99
San Patricio church, 49, 50
Scalfari, Eugenio, 117, 130
Scherer, Pedro Odilo (cardinal), 82
Schmidtner, Johann Georg, 28–29
Schönborn, Christoph (cardinal), 81

Scola, Angelo (cardinal), 82, 91
Second Vatican Council. *See* Vatican II
seminary, 10, 11, 18, 47, 59–60
September 11 attacks, 41–42
sexual abuse scandal, 62, 71, 81, 111, 120, 128–30
Sistine Chapel, 66, 67, 76, 83, 84, 86, 91, 94
Sivori, Francisco (uncle), 6
Sivori, Regina María (mother), 5–6, 8, 10–11, 12, 18, 28
Skorka, Abraham (rabbi), 55–56, 59–60, 62, 125, 126
social justice, 23–25, 113, 116–17, 119, 121, 124, 127. *See also* poor
Society of Jesus. *See* Jesuit Order
Sodano, Angelo (cardinal), 77, 78, 85, 99
South Korea, 132
Spadero, Antonio, 115
Spain, Madrid, 18
speeches, 54, 57, 58, 80, 96, 98, 106, 109, 113, 118. *See also* preaching/homilies
spirituality, 10, 17, 28–29, 38, 53, 90, 92, 98, 101, 118
St. Anna church, 95
St. John Lateran Basilica, 107
St. Mary Major, Basilica of, 15, 92
St. Peter am Perlach church, 28–29
St. Peter's Basilica, 65, 66, 77, 78, 87, 91, 104, 105, 107, 122

St. Peter's Square, 64, 67, 68, 77, 84, 86, 98, 102, 103, 108, 116, 125

St. Robert Bellarmine, Church of, 41

Swindon, Andres, 27

Syria, 116, 125, 126

Tagle, Luis Antonio (cardinal), 76, 82

Tauran, Jean Louis (cardinal), 86, 88

Tebartz-van Elst, Franz-Peter (bishop), 123–24

Toledo, Roberto, 39

United States, 21, 47, 62, 72, 135–36. *See also* September 11 attacks

University of Alcalá de Henares de Madrid, 18

Vallini, Agostino (cardinal), 77, 91, 105, 121

Vatican, 40–42, 69, 71–72, 74, 75, 77, 79, 95–96, 97. *See also* pope, election process/ conclave for; St. Peter's Square

Vatican II, 18–19, 20, 24, 28, 42, 60, 69, 111, 125

Venables, Gregory (bishop), 55

Videla, Jorge (president), 22, 27

Vigano, Carlo Maria (bishop), 72

vocation. *See under* Jesuit Order and Bergoglio/Francis

Wojtyla, Karol (cardinal). *See* John Paul II

women in the church, 65, 79, 110, 115, 121, 127, 131

World War I, 3, 133

World War II, 19, 21, 55, 64– 65, 127

World Youth Day, 102, 114, 131

Yorio, Orlando, 25–27

youth, Bergoglio's, 6–12

youth and Pope Francis, 92, 105, 106, 108, 112–13, 114, 115, 117, 120–21, 122, 132

Zorin, Victor, 29